FORGED IN FREEDOM

This volume is dedicated
In loving honor of the
Birth
of
Benjamin Cohen Katz
son of
Joanne Louise Cohen
and Aaron David Katz
March 15, 2000
by
Goldie (ל"ז) and Abram Cohen (ל"ז)
Betty Ann (ל"ז) and D. Walter Cohen
Josephine Cohen
Amy Sue Cohen
Jane and Martin Millner
Rachel, Lauren and Michael Millner

FORGED IN FREEDOM

SHAPING THE JEWISH-AMERICAN EXPERIENCE

NORMAN H. FINKELSTEIN

2002 · 5762

The Jewish Publication Society

Philadelphia

The Jewish Publication Society
2100 Arch Street, 2nd floor
Philadelphia, PA 19103

Design and composition by Sandy Freeman

Manufactured in the United States of America

02 03 04 05 06 07 08 09 10   10 9 8 7 6 5 4 3 2 1

Library of Congress Cataloging-in-Publication Data

Finkelstein, Norman H.
    Forged in freedom : shaping the Jewish-American experience / by Norman H. Finkelstein.
        p. cm.
    Summary: A history in words and photographs of the growth of the Jewish community in the United States and its contributions to American culture, politics, and economics in the twentieth century.
    Includes bibliographical references and index.
    ISBN 0-8276-0748-2
    1. Jews—United States—History—Juvenile literature. 2. United States—Ethnic relations—Juvenile literature. [1. Jews—United States—History. 2. Judaism. 3. Ethnic relations.]
    I. Title
        E184.35.F56 2002
        973.04'924—dc21

2002000453

Contents

Acknowledgments . . . vii

Introduction . . . xi

CHAPTER 1   Reforming Judaism:
             The Legacy of the "Treif Banquet" . . . 1

CHAPTER 2   Labor and Justice:
             The Triangle Shirtwaist Company Fire . . . 17

CHAPTER 3   In Unity There Is Strength:
             Lessons from the Kehillah Experiment . . . 37

CHAPTER 4   Fighting Bigotry:
             The Lynching of Leo Frank . . . 57

CHAPTER 5   Creating American Culture:
             The Jazz Singer, Gershwin and Greenberg . . . 79

CHAPTER 6   From *Heder* to Harvard:
The Lesson of Henrietta Szold . . . 103

CHAPTER 7   Years of Despair:
The Riegner Telegram . . . 117

CHAPTER 8   American Jews and Israel:
The Six-Day War and New Relationships . . . 137

CHAPTER 9   Toward Religious Equality for Woman and Gays:
The Ordination of Sally Priesand . . . 153

CHAPTER 10   Coming of Age Politically:
The Selection of Joseph Lieberman . . . 163

CHAPTER 11   Facing the Future:
Where Are We? Where Are We Headed? . . . 181

Notes . . . 191

Timeline . . . 197

Selected Bibliography . . . 199

Index . . . 201

Acknowledgments

I am grateful to many for making this book possible, especially:

Dr. Murray Tuchman and the staff of the Hebrew College Library.

Jane Barowitz of the Jewish Child Care Association of New York.

Susan M. Melnick, Archivist, Historical Society of Western Pennsylvania.

Bruce Black, former editor at The Jewish Publication Society, whose vision inspired the concept, and Dr. Ellen Frankel for her invaluable insight.

My agent, Tracey Adams at McIntosh & Otis.

As always, I am indebted to my wife, Rosalind, for her continued under-standing and advice and to my children, Jeffrey, Jennifer, Robert and Risa, and my grandchildren, Tova and Joseph, for their support.

NHF

For

JOSEPH NOAM FINKELSTEIN

Born in 2000: A Jew and an American

Introduction

In 1998, Joseph Lieberman rose from his seat in the United States Senate to tell his colleagues about his grandmother:

I think of my grandmother, on this day, who came here from Central Europe. My grandmother was probably one of the greatest American patriots I ever knew. And for simple reasons. She said to me one day in her old age how much she loved the country. And she said, "You know, it may not seem that profound to you, it may not seem that complicated . . . But the fact that I can walk to synagogue on Saturday morning and not only is no one harassing me or bothering me or not only do I live free of fear, not only do I have no hesitation about what I will find in the synagogue and no one bothering the building or any of us worshiping there . . . But my neighbors who are not Jewish, as they see me, say, 'Good morning, Mrs. Manger. Good Sabbath to you.'" This to her expressed the essence of what it meant to be American, and free, and the gratitude that she felt.

Mrs. Manger could never have imagined that in the year 2000 her grandson would be the Democratic Party candidate for Vice President of the

United States. Her family's American journey typified the experience of other American Jews. In one hundred years, they had transformed themselves from insecure Yiddish-speaking immigrants into fully participating members of American society. In so doing, they reshaped their Eastern European culture and religion to fit democratic America. And in many ways, big and small, they, in turn, influenced the American lifestyle.

This book traces the cultural, religious and political evolution of Jews in America. It's an exciting story! Let's discover how a series of seemingly unconnected turning points in the twentieth century shaped today's American Jewish community.

Reforming Judaism:
The Legacy
of the "Treif Banquet"

*"Jewish life cannot
be about fighting
assimilation:
It has to be about
something else.
Being Jewish
today means a lot
of different things.
There is this
incredible diversity
of how Jews
define, practice,
believe."*

JONATHAN
WOOCHER

F or the nearly two million Jewish immigrants who came to America one hundred years ago there was but one Judaism: the traditional Orthodoxy of Eastern Europe. Even the nonobservant among them knew the basics. They read Hebrew, understood the rituals and were surrounded by familiar religious customs.

In Europe, Jews, observant or not, were identified by their religion. But in America Jewish immigrants were classified by country of origin and not religion. Although government statistics indicated large numbers of arrivals from Russia and Eastern Europe at the turn of the century, there was no official tally of the numbers of immigrants who were Jewish.

In Eastern Europe, Jews were largely a people apart. They were separated from their non-Jewish neighbors by distinct language, dress, culture, religion and rampant anti-Semitism. While Jews in Western Europe had been slowly assimilated into their countries

Seeking freedom. When the first Jewish settlers arrived in New Amsterdam in 1654, they were met with intolerance. They fought for their rights and prevailed. They established the first synagogue on American soil and became active participants in the life of their community. Their balance of citizenship and religious practice became the model for future Jewish immigrants to the United States. *(New York Public Library Picture Collection)*

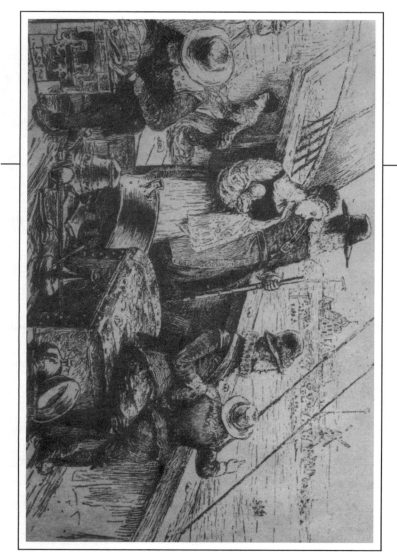

of residence beginning in the eighteenth century, in Russia, Poland and other Eastern European countries, Jews were not considered Russians or Poles; they were simply Jews.

Italian, Irish and Greek Americans gaze back with fondness upon their ancestral lands, but Jews have retained no such attachment to the countries in which their families lived for centuries. Rather, they focus on the isolated Jewish lives of their ancestors. Most Jews living in the shtetl (hamlet) lands of Eastern Europe knew more about the geography of Israel than they did about towns and rivers just miles from their homes.

The Judaism of Eastern Europe was traditional Orthodoxy. Whether Jews were religiously observant or not, their lives revolved around the cycle of religious holidays, life events and customs. The language of Russian Jews was not Russian; of Polish Jews, not Polish; of Lithuanian Jews, not Lithuanian. Wherever Jews lived in Europe, the language that united them was Yiddish. It was this language and its culture that the massive wave of Eastern European immigrants brought with them to America.

When the first Jewish immigrants to America landed in New Amsterdam in 1654, there were just twenty-three of them. Today the number of Jews in the United States stands at six million, the largest Jewish population of any country in the world—including Israel. The change in numbers was accompanied by changes in religious practice. From 1654 until the mid-nineteenth century, Jewish worship in the New World followed the Sephardic traditions that the original settlers brought with them from Spanish and Portuguese lands.

Judaism American Style

The arrival of large numbers of Jewish immigrants from Germany in the mid-nineteenth century changed the character of Jewish religious practice in America. They brought with them a liberal form of religious practice based on a European, or Ashkenazic, form of Judaism. Reform Judaism began in Germany as a reaction to the newly gained political and social freedom of Jews in Germany. It was based on the teachings of Moses Mendelssohn, who in the eighteenth century wrote that Jews should "adopt the mores and constitution of the country in which you find yourself, but be steadfast in upholding the religions of your fathers, too. Bear both burdens as well as you can."[1]

Mendelssohn believed that the existing structures of Judaism could survive intact as the Jews assimilated into the culture around them, but by the turn of the nineteenth century, some rabbis realized that

Mendelssohn's noble intentions could not work on a practical level. Jewish religious practices had to be adapted to make them acceptable to Jews who wanted to become part of the larger world.

The first changes made by the early reforming rabbis were limited. German language was added to the service. Some repetitious prayers were eliminated from the prayer book. Organ music was introduced. The services were made more attractive. In time, other rabbis went further. They debated the use of Hebrew language in Jewish prayers, the role of traditional rituals in Jewish life and the place of kashrut (eating kosher food). These debates were brought to America, where, in the words of the Jewish poet Judah Leib Gordon, one could be "a Jew in his tent and a man abroad."

Reform Judaism in America did not speak with one voice. As in Europe, there were Reform congregations that adhered to a traditional form of worship. In more liberal congregations, men and women sat together, rather than follow the tradition of separating the sexes during services. Other congregations eliminated one day of holiday observance or negated kashrut rules. Over the years, in a series of conferences, the Reform movement issued and refined its official Declaration of Principles. The 1885 Pittsburgh Conference stated that such traditional practices as kashrut, the wearing by men of *kippot* (head coverings) and *tallitot* (prayer shawls) were "entirely foreign to our present mental and spiritual state." The Declaration also stated that Jews were not a separate nation but a "religious community" in America that need not strive for a return to Palestine. The majority had spoken, but not all members of the Reform community were in total agreement.

In spite of the differences that separated opposing wings of the Reform movement, the Union of American Hebrew Congregations (UAHC, the organization to which most Reform congregations belong) was founded in 1873, and then in 1875, Hebrew Union College. The mission of the college was to prepare American-trained rabbis to lead American congregations. Until then, all rabbis in America, Reform and Orthodox, were European-born.

The Birth of the Conservative Movement

Today, we take for granted that American Judaism is divided into three main branches: Orthodox, Conservative and Reform. It was not always so. Until the 1880s, Reform was the dominant Jewish religious movement in America. Massive immigration of Jews from Russia and Eastern Europe at the turn of the twentieth century changed this.

The new immigrants differed markedly from Jews already settled in the United States. They were largely Orthodox, Yiddish-speaking and traditional in religious practice. Even the nonobservant among them knew about religious customs and practices. But they were poor and unfamiliar with Western ways. At first, the established Jewish community tried to distance itself from the newcomers, afraid that other Americans would categorize all Jews together in a wave of discrimination. But blood was thicker than water, and the wealthy German-Jewish community quickly set to work to "Americanize" the latest wave of immigrants.

Three things were clear from the beginning. First, the newcomers would not become Reform Jews. Likewise, the assimilated Reform Jews were not interest-

A street scene of the Jewish Lower East Side of New York at the turn of the twentieth century. The teeming streets bustled with Jewish life. The language was Yiddish but the goal was to "make it in America." (YIVO Institute for Jewish Research)

ed in welcoming these new immigrants to their synagogues. Second, America, with its freedoms and opportunities, would lure the children of the immigrants away from "Old World" Orthodoxy and perhaps Judaism. Finally, Reform Jews were in the process of an identity crisis, as liberals and traditionalists competed for ideological control of their movement. The solution to these problems pointed to the need for a new stream in Judaism that could combine aspects of traditional, familiar observance with an American twist.

For many Jews, a customary way of celebrating an important event is with food. Shabbat dinners and Passover seders are two examples. So, to celebrate the first graduation of American-trained Reform rabbis from Hebrew Union College, guests were invited to a banquet in July 1883, in a Cincinnati hotel. The gaiety of the evening was quickly shattered when the guests sat down to a gourmet meal. The fancy menu included some obviously nonkosher delicacies. Shrimp and crabmeat appetizers were followed by meat and ice cream courses. Some bewildered guests left the room in disgust while others sat in their places not daring to touch the food before them. The liberals in the movement had made their point. There was no place in their vision of Reform Judaism for those who wanted to hold on to old traditions. The "Treif [nonkosher] Banquet," as it came to be known, triggered the development of a new, uniquely American form of Judaism.

In 1902, a group of wealthy Reform Jews invigorated a small, struggling seminary for the training of American rabbis with a sizable contribution. Their foresight established the Jewish Theological Seminary as the fountainhead of the Conservative movement. Today, the quadrangle at the Seminary in New York contains a number of brick columns bearing the names of benefactors, many of whom were Reform Jews.

But it wasn't only the Reform movement that helped build Conservative Judaism in America. The Orthodox community also played a role, though less dramatic and less obvious. The Orthodox population grew dramatically with the arrival of two million Jewish immigrants from Eastern Europe between 1881 and 1914.

The newcomers, Yiddish-speaking and mainly unfamiliar with American culture and traditions, formed a close-knit community based on family, friends and synagogue. The first generation of immigrants quickly discovered that the streets of America were not paved with gold. They also discovered that to succeed in America they needed to adapt to the majority culture.

When faced with the choice of observing the Sabbath or feeding their families, many newcomers were forced to work on Saturdays. Synagogue attendance fell sharply. Jewish education became secondary as parents strove to Americanize their children. They took full advantage of the free and open public school system. It was a time where it was said that the children raised the parents rather than the other way around. In the novel *The Rise of David Levinsky*, by Abraham Cahan, the recent immigrant explains, "If you are a Jew of the type to which I belonged when I came to New York and you attempt to bend your religion to the spirit of your new surroundings, it breaks. It falls to pieces. The very clothes I wore and the very food I ate had a fatal effect on my religious habits." A prominent European rabbi, alarmed at what was happening to traditional religious practices, urged Jews not to immigrate to America. It was, he declared, a "*treif*" land.

Conservative Judaism, a legacy of the Treif Banquet, offered American-born children of immigrants a way to preserve their religious heritage while becoming part of American life. In Conservative temples, the rituals, prayers and *halakhah* (Jewish religious law) were adapted to fit the American lifestyle.

As economic conditions improved, families moved from the crowded city ghettos. In New York, by the 1930s, the majority of Jews lived outside the Lower East Side in Brooklyn or the Bronx, in what was then referred to as "the country." This process was repeated elsewhere. In Boston, the shift from Roxbury, Chelsea and Dorchester led to the suburbs of Brookline, Newton and Swampscott. In Pittsburgh, children of immigrants left the crowded downtown sections for the serenity of Squirrel Hill. In Baltimore, they moved north to Pikesville. A generation later, their children continued the trek by moving even farther away into the suburbs. Wherever they went, each succeeding generation built new synagogue buildings for their old congregations or established new houses of worship.

The Different Faces
of Orthodox Judaism

By the 1930s, the Orthodox community in the United States was in "an advanced state of break-down."[2] This was brought about by the passing of the original immigrant generation, severe limitation on the numbers of new immigrants into the country by the government and the growth of Conservative and Reform Judaism. What's more, Orthodox Jews were not immune from the Americanization trends adopted by the more liberal branches of Judaism. Many younger members did not feel at home in the Yiddish-speaking, "old-world" surroundings of the typical Orthodox synagogue.

In 1912, a small group of young Orthodox Jews founded the National Council of Young Israel to advance "traditional Torah-true" Judaism. Their goal was to "instill into American Jewish youth an understanding and appreciation of the high ethical and spiritual values of Judaism and demonstrate the compatibility of the ancient faith of Israel with good Americanism."[3] Their attempt to create a "modern Orthodoxy" in America succeeded in stemming the flow away from traditional Judaism. Today, there are over one hundred Young Israel congregations and other modern Orthodox congregations in the United States, which allow their members to successfully meld traditional Jewish practice with secular careers and lives.

Yet, through most of the twentieth century, the Orthodox in America were concerned about being swallowed up by the surrounding culture. In 1923, they began raising funds to establish a university that encompassed both secular and Jewish learning. The new university was built in a choice uptown Manhattan neighborhood in order to move Orthodox Judaism "out of the ghettos where it is now hidden and confined." When Yeshiva University was formally opened in 1929, a Yiddish newspaper called it a "celebration of the victory of traditional Judaism over the spirit of reform and secularism that exists in our land." Modern Orthodoxy permitted young people to live a traditional Jewish life while partaking of the "American dream." In the 1950s, under the leadership of the great talmudic scholar Rabbi Joseph B. Soloveitchik day schools were established where, breaking with tradition, boys and girls studied together in the same classes. This relaxation of strict interpretation of Jewish religious practice, while welcomed by many, did not meet universal acceptance in the Orthodox world.

The arrival of Orthodox immigrants following the Holocaust transformed the American Orthodox community. The newcomers were less willing to adopt American ways and concentrated almost exclusively on their own

Reaching Out

The 1990 National Jewish Population Study yielded disturbing information. Of the nearly 5.6 million Jews in North America, one million did not actively identify themselves as Jews, and over one million rarely attended synagogue and had minimal connection to Jewish life.

To counteract these numbers, the National Jewish Outreach Program in the mid-1990s created the "Shabbat Across America" program. In over 750 congregations of all denominations, on the same well-advertised Friday night, Jewish men, women and children are invited to join together to experience a traditional Shabbat service and dinner. Since the program began, hundreds of thousands of unaffiliated Jews have participated and learned about the importance of Shabbat in Jewish life.

religious and educational objectives. They created schools for their students and restricted contact not only with Reform and Conservative Jews but with modern Orthodox Jews as well. With that rightward move came a stricter Orthodox interpretation of ritual and Jewish law. To the surprise of many, the 1980s saw an upturn in interest by younger Jews in Orthodox Judaism. The new fervor was attributed to the desire of many to seek out a more traditional Jewish lifestyle. But even with this revitalization, American Orthodox Jews, by the year 2000, made up less than 10 percent of the total American Jewish population.

Change and Controversy

Although their numbers are small in comparison with Reform and Conservative Jews, Orthodox Judaism has had an influence on the more liberal Jewish groups. By the end of the century, the Reform and Conservative movements witnessed a shift to the right—toward increased acceptance of ritual, prayer and education.

In the 1980s, the Reform movement caused a rift with Orthodox and Conservative Judaism by recognizing as Jewish anyone born of either a Jewish mother or father. Until then, all Jews shared a single legal answer to the question of "who is a Jew?" Anyone born of a Jewish mother or converted to Judaism was recognized as a Jew. Faced with an increasing intermarriage rate and the desire to keep children of such marriages within the Jewish fold, the Reform movement amended the traditional definition to include the child of either a Jewish mother or a Jewish father. This single decision separated Reform Judaism even further from the Jewish mainstream.

Yet, in 1999, when the Reform movement met again in Pittsburgh, they moved away from earlier liberal pronouncements. The delegates reemphasized the importance of traditional religious practice, use of Hebrew language and support of Israel.

The Orthodox world itself was not immune from a growing separation between its modern Orthodox wing and members who were more traditional. Under the slogan "The Courage to Be Modern and Orthodox," a conference of concerned Orthodox Jews gathered in 1999 to evaluate their positions. They were concerned with the isolationist tendencies within Orthodoxy that separated them not only from Reform and Conservative Jews but even from other Orthodox Jews.

In a 1997 news conference, a small but vocal group of Orthodox rabbis stated that "Reform and Conservative Judaism are not Judaism at all. They are outside of Torah and outside of Judaism." Simultaneously, a legal question thousands of miles away in Israel heightened tensions even more. Proposals were introduced in the Knesset, Israel's parliament, to amend the right of any Jew to seek Israeli citizenship by banning anyone converted by Conservative or Reform rabbis. Only people converted by Orthodox rabbis would be recognized as Jews. On the surface, the proposal seemed to target a relatively small number of converts, but the obvious agenda was to delegitimize Conservative and Reform rabbis and, by association, a majority of American Jews.

Assimilation and Identity

The move from urban to suburban living heightened the role of the synagogue in the lives of American Jews. In the larger cities at the turn of the century, it was not difficult for a Jew to find connections to a Jewish life. Wherever one turned there were Yiddish conversations, synagogues, kosher restaurants and Jewish neighbors. No one needed to belong to a synagogue or check a calendar to know it was Shabbat or Yom Kippur or Passover.

In the suburbs, where Jews were not in the majority, joining a temple defined one's Judaism. Reform and Conservative temples flourished: many people flocked to them not only to fulfill religious needs but also to provide for their social needs. As the century ended, the freedoms of America had allowed most Jews to forget the past fears that had united them. Gone were fears of anti-Semitism, concern for Israel's survival and immediate memories of the Holocaust. Coupled with minimal attachment to religious practice, Jews found they truly lived lives governed by choice, and one of the choices was not to be religiously observant.

As Jews became better educated, financially secure and assimilated into American life, they began to create individual Jewish identities not always centered on a house of worship. Beginning in the 1960s, Jewish families unhappy with the impersonal nature of large temples created *havurot*, small groups that allowed members to personalize prayer and enjoy Jewish fellowship. The members created their own services and creatively celebrated life-cycle events and holidays.

14

Interior of Wald's Grocery Store, Murray Avenue, Pittsburgh, Pennsylvania, 1923. Corner "mom-and-pop" grocery stores in America's cities served the needs of immigrant neighborhoods. The owners, like their customers, spoke Yiddish, and they extended credit to families with no money. *(Rauh Archives, Historical Society of Western Pennsylvania)*

A 1999 Gallup Poll on religion in America discovered that Jews were "the least religious," with only 30 percent of them saying that their religion was very important to them. Dr. Gary Tobin, a scholar of Jewish religion, responded that "Jews tend to say I'm not very religious, which means I'm not very observant. It doesn't mean they don't care about being Jewish."[4]

Rabbi Jerome Epstein, a leader in the Conservative movement, argued, "We don't talk about God enough." The goal of Jewish religious leaders at the end of the century was to bring "two- or three-day-a-year Jews" back to synagogue life.

To break the cycle of decreasing religious observance, many innovative programs have been developed to bring Jews back to religion. "Shabbat Across America" utilized the latest advertising techniques, including radio jingles, to urge Jews across the country to celebrate Shabbat on specific Friday nights at local synagogues. Shabbat observance has been part of the Jewish experience for over five thousand years, and making it a pleasant, positive event might be a way of influencing Jews to participate in other religious activities. The Hebrew writer Ahad Ha'am put it this way: "As much as the Jews have kept the Sabbath, the Sabbath has kept the Jewish people."

The twentieth century was a period of momentous upheaval and change for Jews worldwide. The Holocaust and the reestablishment of a Jewish homeland after two thousand years deeply affected Jewish identity. For many, that identity evolved outside of the synagogue. Commitment to Jewish causes rose as attendance at synagogue dropped. Jews turned their

President Calvin Coolidge speaking at the cornerstone dedication of the Jewish Community Center, Washington, D.C., 1925. The appearance of important public figures at Jewish events provided Jews with a sense of acceptance and pride. *(Library of Congress)*

By the Numbers

The 1990 National Jewish Population Survey totaled 5,515,000 Jews in North America. Those who were religiously connected identified themselves as:

Reform	41.4 percent
Conservative	40.4 percent
Orthodox	6.8 percent
"Just Jewish"	5.2 percent
Other	6.2 percent

energies into support for Holocaust education, combating anti-Semitism and discrimination, fundraising and political lobbying for Israel.

The birthrate of American Jews fell as the intermarriage rate rose. Toward the end of the twentieth century, with Israel strong and self-sufficient, American Jews began to look inward at the problems they faced at home: intermarriage, education and identity.

CHAPTER 2

Labor and Justice:
The Triangle Shirtwaist
Company Fire

F or many Jews, the long immigrant journey to America ended with a short walk up Broadway to New York's Lower East Side. There, amid crowded buildings and vibrant streets, they hoped to find opportunity and freedom. But their dreams of a land where the "streets were paved with gold" quickly evaporated into bleak reality. Unskilled and uncertain of the English language, they desperately searched for jobs to keep their families alive. "Their sweatshops," wrote Jacob Riis, "and their starvation wages, are the faithful companions of their dire poverty."[1]

Many children, after a full day at school, rushed home to help mothers, brothers and sisters with "piecework" until late at night to supplement the family income. In many households, a young schoolgirl became the "little mother" to her younger brothers and sisters while their mother worked the night shift as a cleaner in a midtown office building. Others were unable to even think of attending school. In 1901, an estimated sixty

"They say a day has 24 hours. That's a bluff. A day has 12 coats . . . I still have two coats to make of the 12 that I got yesterday. So it's still Monday, with me. My Tuesday won't begin before about 2 o'clock this afternoon.

FROM A
SWEATSHOP
ROMANCE,
BY ABRAHAM
CAHAN

17

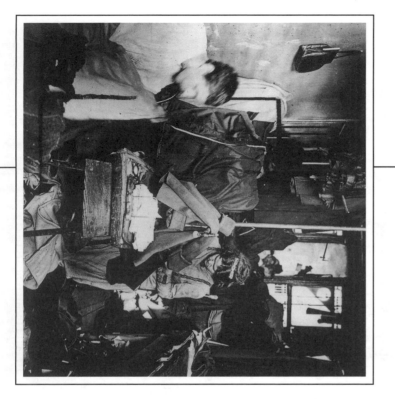

thousand New York children were shut up in home "sweatshops." "Many of this immense host will never sit on a school bench. Is it not a cruel civilization that allows little hearts and little shoulders to strain under these grown-up responsibilities?" asked one reformer.

Behind the thin, paint-peeling tenement walls, most families struggled just to survive. Finding a job was not difficult, but the low wages and long working hours took their toll on home life. Fathers and mothers who worked had little time to spend with their families.

The only jobs available for many men and women were in the area's many garment factories, some nothing more than sectioned-off rooms in walk-up tenement buildings. Earlier arrivals, having met with some financial success, opened factories in large buildings that employed more recent immigrants. Cold in winter, hot in summer, these factories were dirty, noisy and unhealthy. Windows and doors were often locked shut to prevent thefts. The closed windows also kept out fresh air, and, as a result, many workers developed lifelong sicknesses. It didn't take workers long to discover why their factories were known as "sweatshops." The women workers, most of them young and unmarried, were paid less than men and usually worked twelve- to fourteen-hour days, six days a week.

There was little time for fun. "All week long I wouldn't see the daylight," Clara Lemlich remembered. "The shops are unsanitary—that's the word that is generally used, but there ought to be a worse one used."[2] Anyone who spoke to the boss about working conditions could be fired on the spot and instantly replaced by newer immigrants. "In the shops we don't have names, we have numbers," one woman said. Yet few workers complained. They considered themselves fortunate to have jobs at all!

At the end of a long and tiring week, workers did not even receive the full amount of the low pay they had earned. Deducted from their wages were charges for sewing needles and use of the building's electricity and storage lockers. Some bosses even charged workers for sitting on the factory's stools!

Workers Unite

I n 1900, workers in garment factories decided to unite and fight for their rights. Many of them were Jewish. Although most were not religious, they lived in Jewish environments, spoke Yiddish and understood Jewish customs and culture. They had brought with them from Europe a tradition of socialist activism. "In unity there is strength," they told each other. They founded the ILGWU, the International Ladies Garment

(Photo at right) Garment workers parading on May Day in New York, 1916. Job opportunities for recent immigrants were limited. Poor working conditions and low wages led many to join unions. Banded together, they fought for and won improved conditions in their shops. (*Library of Congress*)

Workers Union. Clara Lemlich became an active union supporter, described by a union leader as "a pint of trouble for the bosses."

In September 1909, Clara and other women could no longer tolerate their harsh working conditions. They walked out of the Leiserson factory and went on strike. Within a few days the strike spread to the workers at the nearby Triangle Shirtwaist Company.

Day after day the young women strikers picketed the factories to let the public know they were on strike and to prevent replacement workers from entering the factories. They walked up and down the sidewalk in front of the buildings; some carried signs while others chanted and sang.

The factory owners hired gangs of tough men to frighten the pickets. As the mostly Jewish and Italian teenage girls peacefully walked the picket lines they were threatened and pushed by the ruffians. Women were beaten, punched and thrown to the ground. Many were badly hurt. The police did little to prevent the violence. Day after day the strikers endured blows from the hoodlums while Clara and other union supporters encouraged them to keep up their spirits by singing Italian and Yiddish songs. "Stand fast, girls," Clara told them. During one attack in mid-November Clara and two other young women were so badly beaten the police had to rush them to a hospital.

Eleven weeks after walking out of the Leiserson and Triangle companies, the women workers saw no end to the bloody strike. While they were on strike they earned no money, and the poor women faced a harsh, hungry and cold winter. Union leaders realized that the only quick way to improve working conditions and wages was to shut down every shirtwaist factory in New York.

On November 22, 1909, thousands of shirtwaist workers gathered in the Cooper Union Auditorium. It was time to make a decision. Should all the shirtwaist work-

ers in the city go out on strike? Clara and her friends pushed their way through the throngs to better see and hear the famous speakers. Around them, they heard the voices of concerned women:

"What happens if we go on strike?"

"Who knows how many workers will participate?"

"Who can tell how long it will last?"

The audience cheered a succession of speakers, finally focusing their attention on Samuel Gompers, the best-known speaker of the evening. He was the founder and president of America's most powerful union, the American Federation of Labor. Gompers was a Jewish immigrant who came to the United States with his parents during the Civil War. Like his father, he became a cigar maker and joined the Cigarmaker's Union. Gompers quickly rose through the union ranks, and in 1886 he organized a number of independent unions into the American Federation of Labor.

Speaking in Yiddish, Gompers told the excited crowd, "I say, friends, do not enter too hastily but when you can't get the manufacturers to give you what you want, then strike. And when you strike, let the manufacturers know you are on strike!" He concluded by urging his listeners "to stand together, to have faith in yourselves, to be true to your comrades. If you strike, be cool, calm, collected and determined. Let your watchword be: Union and progress, and until then no surrender!"[3]

After two hours of cautious speeches with no end in sight, "a thin wisp of a girl" asked to speak. As she stepped onto the platform, the crowd quieted. Everyone knew Clara Lemlich, the brave union worker who had just been released from the hospital. She still showed signs of the violent beating she received on the picket line. Her words, spoken in clear and passionate Yiddish, echoed through the hall. It was a clarion call to action.

"I have listened to all the speakers, and I have no further patience for talk. I am a working girl, one of those

Reforming the Sweatshop

Social workers and reformers of the time documented the terrible working conditions in the sweatshops. They hoped to encourage public indignation and enact strict labor laws.

One report from 1906 details the working conditions in a bindery sweatshop:

They begin at 8 in the morning.
They do not stop working until 10 o'clock at night.
They have a half-hour for dinner and half-hour for supper.
They work 13 hours a day, 78 hours a week.
Wages were $6 a week. They would "probably" be discharged if they refused to work overtime.[4]

striking against intolerable conditions. I am tired of listening to speakers who talk in generalities. What we are here for is to decide whether or not to strike. I offer a resolution that a general strike be declared—now!"

The audience erupted into wild applause. People jumped from their seats, cheered and waved handkerchiefs. This was the moment they had waited for. For five minutes, the chairman banged his gavel for order. "Will you take the old Jewish oath?" he shouted over the noise of the excited crowd. The room stilled for a brief moment. Then, two thousand workers raised their hands and recited, "If I turn traitor to the cause I now pledge, may this hand wither from the arm I now raise."

On Strike!

Within two days the entire shirtwaist industry in New York City was shut down. No one had predicted the resolve of the strikers. Twenty thousand workers, mainly Jewish and Italian teenage girls and young women, marched in picket lines before factories throughout lower Manhattan. The police did little to prevent violence against them. When arrests were made, it was usually those picketing who were taken off to court. Through the barred police wagon windows, women under arrest shouted to their friends, "Do not lose courage; we will win yet!"

In the first month of the strike, over seven hundred pickets were arrested. The judges showed no mercy. "You have no right to picket!" one judge said. Twenty young women workers were sentenced to jail, where they were forced to mingle with common criminals. One teenage girl was sent to jail for five days when she complained that a police officer was hitting strikers. "There was never anything like it . . . an equal number of men would never hold together under what these girls are enduring," one union man said.

Newspapers widely reported on the brutality against the strikers. Other women, wealthy and educated, decided to prevent the brutality and unfair arrests. With great publicity, they joined the poorly dressed and ill-fed immigrant women workers on the picket lines. When one of the volunteers was arrested and brought to court, a police officer apologized, "Why didn't you tell me you was a rich lady? I'd never have arrested you in the world!"

The society women picketed city hall to protest unfair police treatment of the workers. They marched with signs that read, "Peaceful picketing is the right of every woman!" Famous women and students from respected women's colleges raised thousands of dollars to help the poor strikers survive. When the weather grew bitterly cold, the rich women set up soup kitchens to provide the skimpily dressed picketers with hot meals.

The brave struggle of Clara Lemlich and the other women workers is known as the "Uprising of the Twenty Thousand." By February 15, 1910, it was over. The strikers won a shorter workweek of fifty-two hours, higher wages and the end of unfair deductions for supplies, chairs and lockers. Sadly, they did not gain other demands for improved safety conditions such as unlocked exit doors and easy approaches to fire escapes.

By the end of the strike over ten thousand workers had joined the ILGWU. The "Uprising of the Twenty Thousand" was the largest strike of women to date. As one participant said, "This is not just a strike for self. Only by standing together can we get better conditions for all." Clara Lemlich later recalled, "They used to say that you couldn't even organize women. Well, we showed them!" The unity and determination of Clara and the other women led to the success and inspired other workers to fight for their rights.

Later in 1910, a larger strike of sixty thousand mostly male New York cloakmakers, known as "The Great Revolt," almost brought the American garment industry to a complete stop. Leaders of the American Jewish community were concerned with the bitter confrontation between Jewish bosses and Jewish workers. Boston lawyer Louis D. Brandeis worked out a settlement. A few years later he became the first Jewish justice of the United States Supreme Court.

Life in the Shop

Clara Lemlich vividly described her working life in this article, which appeared on November 28, 1909, in *The New York Evening Journal*:

"First let me tell you something about the way we work and what we are paid. There are two kinds of work—regular, that is salary work, and piecework. The regular work pays about $6 a week and the girls have to be at their machines at 7 o'clock in the morning and they stay at them until 8 o'clock at night, with just one-half hour for lunch in that time.

"The shops. Well, there is just one row of machines that the daylight ever gets to—that is the front row, nearest the window. The girls at all the other rows of machines back in the shops have to work by gaslight, by day as well as by night. Oh, yes, the shops keep the work going at night, too.

"The bosses in the shops are hardly what you would call educated men, and the girls to them are part of the machines they are running. They yell at the girls and they 'call them down' even worse than I imagine Negro slaves were in the South.

"There are no dressing rooms for the girls in the shops. They have to hang up their hats and coats—such as they are—on hooks along the walls. Sometimes a girl has a new hat. It never is much to look at because it never costs more than 50 cents; that means that we have gone for weeks on two-cent lunches—dry cake and nothing else.

"The shops are unsanitary—that's the word that is generally used, but there ought to be a worse one used. Whenever we tear or damage any of the goods we sew on, or whenever it is found damaged after we are through with it, whether we have done it or not, we are charged for the piece and sometimes for a whole yard of the material.

"At the beginning of every slow season, $2 is deducted from our salaries. We have never been able to find out what this is for."

The "Protocol of Peace," as the agreement was called, called for joint worker and owner committees to settle grievances. Most important for the union, it provided for a system of "preferential shops" where union members were given preference in hiring and promotion. Thanks to the blood, sweat and tears of Jewish workers, unions become a force in American life. But the struggle was far from over.

The Triangle Fire

The Triangle Shirtwaist Company occupied the top three floors of a ten-floor building in Washington Square, near New York University. It was just before the 5 o'clock quitting time on Saturday afternoon, March 25, 1911, and workers were looking forward to what was left of their short weekend. All of a sudden they smelled smoke; men and women scurried to the nearest exits. As a rule only one exit was available to workers. Pauline Pepi, a survivor, recalled "we never went out the front door. We always went out by one out the back. There was a man there searching because the people were afraid we would take something, so that door was always locked." Other doors were either locked or, because they opened inward, were blocked by the sheer number of workers pressing against them. The sole fire escape was useless; because it was indoors it was quickly engulfed by flames. The only fire prevention tools available were twenty-seven buckets of water.

As the flames and smoke intensified behind them, workers clawed their way to the windows and ledges. Below them, the first fire engines had begun to deploy their hoses and ladders. Unfortunately, both the ladders and streams of water could reach only part way up the building, leaving the terrified workers on the top floors with no hope of escape. "Don't jump!" onlookers below shouted. The frantic young women had no choice. It was jump or be burned.[5]

Frances Perkins, who decades later would become the first woman member of a president's cabinet, happened upon the chaotic scene as "people had just begun to jump . . . they had been holding until that time, standing in the windowsills, being crowded by others behind them, the fire pressing closer and closer, the smoke closer and closer." Firemen held taut blankets and safety nets aloft to catch the jumpers but the bodies hurtled through the blankets as if through paper. Girls fell with "fire streaming back from their hair and dresses," and landed "thud-dead" on the sidewalk.[6] Not a single jumper survived.

Frances Perkins recalled, "The weight of the bodies was so great at the speed at which they were traveling that they broke through the net. Every one of them was killed. Everybody who jumped was killed. It was a horrible spectacle." The loss of life could have been much higher, since the building contained a number of other cloak shops. Fortunately, they were union shops and closed at 1 o'clock on Saturdays, a hard-won benefit to workers of the 1909 shirtwaist strike.

The Lower East Side was enveloped in bitter mourning. Most of the dead were young Jewish and

The Uprising of the Twenty Thousand

In the black of winter of nineteen nine,
When we froze and bled on the picket line,
We showed the world that women could fight.
And we rose and won with women's might.
Hail! The waistmakers of nineteen nine,
Making their stand on the picket line.
Breaking the power of those who reign,
Pointing the way, smashing the chain.
And we gave new courage to the men
Who carried on in nineteen ten
And shoulder to shoulder we'll win through,
Led by the ILGWU.[7]

Honoring the Victims

The building that once housed the Triangle Shirtwaist Company is no more. Today, the site is occupied by a building of New York University. A marker, placed by the ILGWU, now designates the spot of the fire and honors the victims. It reads as follows:

On this site, 146 workers lost their lives in the Triangle Shirtwaist Company fire on March 25, 1911. Out of their martyrdom came new concepts of social responsibility and labor legislation that have helped make American working conditions the finest in the world.

Italian women, recent immigrants. The tragic deaths of 146 young workers enraged public opinion and energized unions. *The Ladies Garment Worker* of April 1911 complained righteously:

Is it not strange that in this most democratic of all countries in the world the employers can so easily use the arm of the law to protect themselves against any inconveniences which their workpeople may cause them, but the law is nowhere when the life and limb of the worker is to be protected.

But this tragedy was too public for the government to ignore.

Jewish Workers and the Unions

Jews were at the forefront in the political activism that followed the Triangle fire. They helped win passage of labor laws, fire-safety rules and workers' compensation plans to protect the lives of all workers. Bowing to the political pressure, the governor of New York appointed a high-profile commission to investigate the tragedy. One of its members was Frances Perkins, the woman who witnessed the fire. The investigation led to the passage of the first major factory safety laws in the United States and some fire-fighting innovations. In the decades that followed, states and the federal government enacted stricter regulations to protect the health and safety of workers. Today, factories must have unlocked and clearly marked exits, sprinkler systems, fire extinguishers and uncluttered passageways.

Anarchist leaders Emma Goldman and Alexander Berkman were convicted of conspiracy against the draft law and sentenced to two years in jail on July 9, 1917. Jewish immigrants brought with them a tradition of liberal political activism. Emma Goldman was a major figure in the history of feminism and radical politics. She fought for equal rights, free speech and the eight-hour workday. Her fight against the conscription of young men into the army just prior to the United States' entry into World War I led to her imprisonment and deportation. *(National Archives)*

By the outbreak of World War I, membership in the unions of the American Federation of Labor exceeded two million. Other unions thrived too. Jewish activists were at the forefront of the nation's liberal social-improvement movements. One of them was David Dubinsky, born in Poland in 1892. As a youth, he became active in socialist organizations. Arrested and sent to Siberia for his efforts in leading a strike, he escaped and made his way to the United States, where he openly joined the Socialist Party and went to work in the garment industry. His idealism led him to union activity and up the ranks of the ILGWU leadership. In 1932, he was elected president. Other leaders, including Rose Schneiderman and Belle Moskowitz, used their labor affiliations to become prominent in national political life.

The Workmen's Circle was founded in New York in 1900 and became the premier organization of the Yiddish-speaking, liberal Jewish community. In its heyday, it had branches in major American cities. Today, its membership has dwindled and changed—most members now are college graduates. What has remained constant is the organization's commitment to civil rights, education, Jewish culture (especially the Yiddish language) and Israel.

With the rise to power of the Nazis in Germany, Jewish labor leaders saw the need to educate the American labor movement and the general public about the looming Nazi threat. In 1934, one thousand delegates from the ILGWU, the Amalgamated Clothing Workers, United Hebrew Trades, Workmen's Circle and the *Forward* newspaper gathered in New York to found the Jewish Labor Committee. Throughout the Holocaust years, the Committee represented Jewish labor interests to the world.

The Growth of Liberalism

The Yiddish-speaking immigrants of the 1900s brought with them a legacy of socialist and revolutionary activism in Europe. One woman who symbolized the extremes of liberal politics was Emma Goldman. She was born in Lithuania in 1869 and moved with her parents to St. Petersburg, Russia, when she was thirteen. There she witnessed the injustices of Russian life and decided to devote her life to creating a world of justice and equality. Rebuffed by her parents, Emma set sail for America.

She soon became a well-known activist, protesting

President Franklin D. Roosevelt. American Jews were nearly unanimous in their support for Roosevelt. His social agenda during the Great Depression appealed to the Jewish community. Although he is credited with successfully directing the defeat of Nazi Germany, some think he could have done more to save European Jews before and during the Holocaust. *(Franklin D. Roosevelt Library)*

against the excesses of the American workplace and surrounding herself in an aura of notoriety. She became the uncrowned leader of the American anarchists who were opposed to all forms of government based on force. "Resistance to tyranny is man's highest ideal," she said. She was a frequent participant in marches, strikes and demonstrations. She crisscrossed the country, speaking on a wide range of issues most Americans preferred not to hear about, including birth control, women's rights and pacifism.

With the outbreak of World War I, Emma Goldman urged young men not to register for the draft. "We Americans," she said, "claim to be a peace-loving people. We hate bloodshed: we are opposed to violence. Yet we go into spasms of joy over the possibility of projecting dynamite bombs from flying machines upon helpless citizens." Her outspoken opposition to the popular war led to her arrest and deportation from the United States. She died in 1940.

Emma Goldman occupied a distinct and provocative niche in the American political spectrum, but most other Jews took less inflammatory routes to political participation. Their experiences with bigotry in Europe and fights for worker rights in America developed into a tradition of supporting liberal causes. When the Great Depression of the 1930s nearly tore America's social fabric apart, President Franklin D. Roosevelt embarked on a revolutionary governmental experiment to reshape the country's economic and social policy. American Jews overwhelmingly embraced Roosevelt and his ideas and became stalwarts of the Democratic Party. In spite of the economic advancements made by Jews since the 1930s, for the most part they have remained loyal to the Democratic Party and its liberal principles. As other groups in the United States became wealthier, they turned more conservative and embraced the Republican Party, but the Jews remained loyal Democrats. In a 1999

Rabbi Abraham Joshua Heschel presenting an award to civil rights leader the Reverend Martin Luther King Jr. The friendship of these two religious leaders symbolized the special relationship that existed between Jews and African-Americans in the decades-long struggle for civil rights. *(Library of Congress)*

survey, over 50 percent of American Jewish voters identified themselves as Democrats; only 12 percent considered themselves Republican.

In the years prior to World War II, Jews were reluctant to call public attention to themselves. This "sha-sha syndrome" (Sha! Keep quiet and don't call attention to yourself) resulted from a fear of unleashing latent anti-Semitism. After the Holocaust and the establishment of the State of Israel, Jews became more politically active. "What we have seen over the past twenty or twenty-five years is Jews coming of age, in a political sense," said Stuart Eizenstat, an undersecretary of commerce in the Clinton administration. "We've become much more vocal, not just as an outside interest group, but by integrating into the system."

Issues such as the separation of church and state, prayer in schools and employment quotas held the interest of Jews. Many Jews considered involvement in civil liberties activities a religious experience. The story, whether true or not, is often told about the wealthy Jewish woman who, when asked how she defined her Judaism answered, "I read *The New York Times!*"

During this time, Jews were in the forefront of civil rights activities and legislation. The ILGWU, with its pre-dominantly Jewish leadership, was at the forefront of welcoming and empowering African-American members in the 1930s and 1940s. Martin Luther King Jr. said, "Probably more than any other ethnic group, the Jewish community has been sympathetic and has stood as an ally to the Negro in his struggle for justice."

The immigrant experience shaped the progressive political views with which most Jews identify today. The Triangle fire provided the spark that drew them actively into the political arena. In less than one hundred years they had moved from unknown behind-the-scenes activists to respected national leaders.

In Unity
There Is Strength:
Lessons from the
Kehillah Experiment

"It is only when all Jews are together as a community that the whole Torah can be fulfilled."

J.M. EPSTEIN

W herever Jews had lived in Europe, whether in backward shtetls or cosmopolitan cities, they tried to lead anonymous lives. Centuries of discrimination and violence had conditioned them to avoid publicity. By not calling attention to themselves, they hoped to avoid the violence and "unpleasantness" of anti-Semitism. Most adhered to the principle of communal responsibility: the shameful act of one Jew was a bad reflection on all Jews. They also established community self-help organizations.

In the early 1900s, the Lower East Side of New York was among the most densely populated places on earth, surpassing even Calcutta, India. Within those crowded blocks, a generation of immigrant Jews endured terrible hardships to see their children realize the goal they themselves never fully reached—becoming "real" Americans.

Today, a summer stroll down Orchard Street provides only a glimpse of what life was like on the Lower

East Side a hundred years ago. Except for the signs over the street level stores, the multistoried brick buildings that line the sun-blocked street have not changed. Pushcarts and open-air stalls no longer compete for precious space, but visitors walk among the remaining street vendors in search of bargains. Today, instead of Yiddish, the languages of the street are more likely to be Spanish or Chinese. The Lower East Side has become the launching site for a new generation of immigrants.

The visitors who roam the Lower East Side today looking for signs of the past carry with them the images

of a world colored more by nostalgia than reality. They imagine a world of hard-working immigrants nurtured in an all-encompassing rich and respected Jewish environment. That memory is only partly correct. It is true that most residents of the Lower East Side were honorable, diligent people. It is also true that within the community there was a strong feeling of solidarity and pride. Yet among the residents were a small number of highly visible criminals and lawbreakers. As their fame grew in the newspaper headlines of the time, they brought shame upon the wider Jewish community.

When parents found it difficult to change their own "old-country" ways, children were caught in a dilemma. Parents wanted their children to become "good" Americans, yet Yiddish was the only language spoken at home. Parents wanted their children to honor the traditional values, but they encouraged them to forgo religious education and aim for university degrees. Over time, parental influence weakened. Young people became interpreters of American culture to their parents and spoke for them at governmental institutions and schools. In many ways, "American" sons and daughters became the parents of their own "foreign" mothers and fathers.

Young people took to the streets, with its constant hurly-burly and excitement. Their own bitterly poor homes afforded little comfort and companionship. Their parents didn't understand them and they, in turn, looked askance upon the parents' "old-fashioned" ways. It was a short trip from the front stoop of their building to the company of other young people also searching for a sense of belonging. For some, the gang took over where family responsibility ended.

Eddie Cantor, from Street Kid to Star

"I know about delinquency," Eddie Cantor once said, "and not from reading books. I lived with it."

His story is typical of the experiences of many young people growing up on New York's Lower East Side. Eddie found himself torn between two worlds. One, founded on family-based immigrant traditions and culture, was familiar yet restrictive. The other, centered on the untamed companionship of the gritty streets, represented freedom and opportunity. For young people seeking a way out of the stifling ghetto, the streets were a convenient means of escape.

Eddie Cantor was born Edward Israel Iskowitz in a

Eddie Cantor. In 1892, Eddie Cantor was born Edward Iskowitz in New York City, to poor Russian-Jewish immigrants. His talent for mimicry led him into vaudeville and then to the Broadway stage and ultimately to radio and television. *(National Archives)*

small gaslit bedroom above a tearoom on January 31, 1892. By the time he was four both his father and mother were dead, and Grandma Esther became the young orphan's mother and father. She was a no-nonsense, hardworking woman who scraped money together so they could both survive. Although the love they shared was deep and heartfelt, the clash of cultures divided them. Esther, Yiddish-speaking and unfamiliar with American ways, quickly lost control of her streetwise, cocky grandson.

School was not one of Eddie's favorite activities. Although he enjoyed participating in school plays, reciting memorized orations before his classmates and embittering the lives of his teachers, he never studied. His school career came to an abrupt end in the eighth grade when he was expelled for throwing a blackboard eraser at a teacher.

Eddie received his real education on the streets of the Lower East Side. By the time he was six years old he was singing on street corners with other boys for the pennies of passersby. But life on the streets had a rough edge, too. Fights were commonplace, and skinny Eddie always found himself in the midst of the action. Once, when he was about nine years old, he was struck in the forehead by a brick during a gang fight. With blood gushing from the deep cut, Grandma Esther carried him to the corner druggist. She didn't believe much in doctors; anyway it cost more to call a real doctor. The druggist, oblivious to sanitary needs, stitched the wound closed.

The infection that resulted even scared hardened Grandma Esther. Eddie ran a high fever and the wound looked ugly. Esther carried the young boy to the Essex Street Dispensary for emergency treatment. The wound was reopened, treated correctly and restitched. At that time, before modern antibiotics and without special care, infection was a common cause of death. For three months, the old woman took the feverish, pain-wracked boy to the Good Samaritan Dispensary for daily treatment. When the infection was finally controlled and the pain had subsided, Eddie was left with a permanent scar on his forehead to remind him of the gang days of his youth.

Even that brush with death could not keep Eddie off the streets. He joined Pock-Faced Sam's gang, hired himself out as a strikebreaker at three dollars a day and took part in numerous gang fights. The sight of the small skinny boy was not very frightening, so young Eddie summoned up all his acting skills. He pulled his cap low over his eyes, wore a baggy sweater to hide his lack of muscle and "made enough facial contortions to scare away all the opponents my pals couldn't lick." On occasion, he even carried a gun for a local gangster.

When Eddie felt hungry he waited outside a corner grocery store for the appearance of a young boy or girl on an errand. Eddie entered with the unsuspecting shopper and while the grocer waited on the paying customer, he shoved fruit and crackers inside his shirt and casually strolled out to enjoy his feast.

His school career over, Eddie got a job in the mailroom of a large Manhattan insurance company. Within two weeks he was fired; the comic antics that entertained the other workers did not impress his bosses. Eddie returned to the streets and a life on the fringes of delinquency.

Eddie's behavior was not unique for a Lower East Side boy of the time. Leaders of the Jewish community, particularly the established "uptowners," were concerned by the growing problems of crime among poor, undereducated Jewish children. To stem that tide of lawlessness they established social service, educational and recreational agencies to serve the community.

One such agency, the Educational Alliance, sponsored a free summer camp in the country for needy

boys, the only cost being one dollar for transportation. For two weeks, the lucky boys were transported from the grimy, asphalt neighborhoods to the fresh air, beauty and healthy meals at Surprise Lake Camp in Cold Springs, New York. It was there, among the towering pine trees and shimmering lakes, that young Edward, the fledgling gangster, became Eddie Cantor, the respected entertainer. The transformation, however, was not instantaneous.

Old habits die hard. During his first days at camp, Eddie stole two blankets from other boys to insure his own warmth at night. Rather than punish the lad, the camp director took Eddie aside and spoke kindly to him about how his misdeed had harmed others. That was the first time anyone other than Grandma Esther had shown him any compassion.

On Saturday nights, as the boys gathered around

the campfire to sing and tell stories, it was Eddie, the natural entertainer, who got all the attention. The tough city boys sat mesmerized as Eddie, his large eyes rolling and bulging for effect, told and retold stories he originally learned in school. Eddie returned to Lake Surprise Camp summer after summer. Each time, his two-week stay was lengthened because he had become the main source of entertainment.

Eddie Cantor's singing, radio, television and film appearances made him one of America's best-known entertainers. He developed a unique performing style. His trademark included prancing around the stage at a fast pace, clapping his hands and singing catchy tunes.

However, Cantor never forgot his roots. He joined President Franklin Roosevelt in founding the March of Dimes to combat polio and when the State of Israel was established in 1948, he was an active supporter and fundraiser.

He died on October 10, 1964. A few months earlier, President Lyndon Johnson had presented him with a service medal in recognition of his service "to the United States and to humanity." For the boy from Eldridge Street, this was his proudest moment.

Harsh Realities

Eddie Cantor's story had a happy ending. The stories of others did not. As early as 1902, seeing that many young people were heading toward lives of crime, the Jewish Protectory and Aid Society was founded to rehabilitate young Jewish men in reform schools and prisons. In 1906, the Society opened the Hawthorne School for boys referred to it by the courts and the police.

Two years later the Society opened the Lakeview Home for girls.

Just south of Delancy Street on New York's Lower East Side one still climbs the short stairway to reach the entrance of the tenement house at 97 Orchard Street. Today, it is the Tenement Museum, but one hundred years ago it was the crowded home of twenty immigrant families.

The daily grind took its toll on the immigrant families. The cement of traditional cultural and religious values broke apart under the stress. Fathers, unable to cope with the changes and demands, deserted their families in increasing numbers. So great was the problem that the

Gangster "Bugsy" Siegel in the custody of United States marshals, 1941. Not all Jews brought pride to their people. Among the most famous Jews during the first half of the twentieth century were a small number of gangsters. Their way out of the ghetto was through violence and crime. Benjamin "Bugsy" Siegel is credited for developing Las Vegas into a gambling and entertainment center. *(Library of Congress)*

Tenement Museum

Living conditions for immigrant families on the Lower East Side were crowded and unhealthy. Today, visitors to New York City can still climb the short stairway to reach the entrance of the tenement house at 97 Orchard Street. One hundred years ago it was the crowded home to twenty families. Today, it is the Tenement Museum. The famous social reformer and photographer Jacob Riis made this observation in 1906:

"The poorer they are, the higher rent do they pay, and the more do they crowd to make it up between them. They brought nothing, neither money nor artisan skill—nothing but their consuming energy . . . for one am a firm believer in this Jew and in his boy. Ignorant they are, but with a thirst for knowledge that surmounts any barrier."

leading Yiddish newspaper, the *Forward*, regularly featured a missing husband and father column with pictures and descriptions of the deserters.

Perhaps the most widely read column in that newspaper was the "Bintel Brief," where editors answered letters from readers who were perplexed, saddened or confused by what was happening to them and their families in America. One 1906 letter indicates the despair felt by some:

Dear Mr. Editor of the Forward:

I read the troubles of family life in your "Bintel Brief" each day very attentively. But my own troubles are so great, so enormous, that I will not even ask for your permission to print my few words in your paper, as others do, but simply, I ask you right on the spot: HELP!"

Your Constant Reader

45

The Judge Cohen basketball team, Pittsburgh, Pennsylvania. For the children of immigrants, sports was a way to actively participate in American life with their Jewish friends. Playing on teams also provided a healthy outlet for children, many of whom lived in crowded cities. *(Rauh Archives, Historical Society of Western Pennsylvania)*

Institutions sponsored by religious and social reform groups already existed, which offered newcomers refuge, comfort and guidance. Community resource centers, such as the Henry Street Settlement founded in 1893 by Lillian Wald, provided a wide array of social, medical and educational services. For adults, English language and job skills classes prepared older immigrants for productive lives in their new land. For young people, there were sports teams, summer camps and educational activities. Although large numbers of children took part in the many clubs and activities, others did not, and the agencies themselves had no cooperative relationships.

Landsmanshaften (self-help organizations) were the first sources of help for the immigrant families. Since there were few government programs in place for those in need, these mutual aid societies were lifelines. Loosely based on geographic ties to home villages in the "Old Country," the *Landsmanshaften* provided members with health insurance, no-interest loans and medical and burial assistance. The comfort of being part of a group where one's language and customs were familiar helped many families through trying periods. For most immigrants, a forbidding wall that was difficult to broach surrounded the larger American culture. The many *Landsmanshaften* helped members find their place in America while allowing them to preserve their Jewish identities. But as successful as they were, they did not present a unified face to the world.

Shamed into Action

I n 1908, Theodore Bingham, Police Commissioner of the City of New York, wrote an article on New York's foreign criminals. "Among the most expert of all the street thieves," he wrote, "are Hebrew boys under sixteen who are brought up to lives of crime." The commissioner's highly publicized attack galvanized the outraged Jewish community. Poor Jews of the Lower East Side were embarrassed; wealthy "uptown" Jews were frightened. They feared that all Jews in America would be seen as promoters of criminal activity. A Yiddish newspaper complained, "We have a million Jews in New York. Where is their power?" Stunned and embarrassed, leaders of the Jewish community responded. They could not stand by while respectable Jews were being tainted by the criminal activities of an infamous few.

Concerned with the diverse problems facing the

newcomers and the lack of a central, accountable method of delivering services, Judah Magnes, a New York Reform rabbi, led the fight to "develop a real Jewish community"[1] that would "encompass the Jewish communal life of New York. Order and coherence would replace the contention and fragmentation." The name they gave this new organization was the Kehillah—the Community—based on the *kehillah* model of many Eastern European Jewish communities familiar to recent immigrants. While the concept came from Europe, the organization's mission was to hasten the integration of the Jewish immigrants into American life. The Kehillah experiment was an attempt by both the wealthy and established "uptown" Jews and the immigrant "downtown" community to join forces.

Bringing the various Jewish groups together was not easy. Louis Marshall, a leader of the "uptowners"—Reform Jews, wealthy, established—blamed the breakup in traditional family structure on the inflexible religious leaders of the "downtowners"—Orthodox, poor, unassimilated. In a letter to Judah Magnes, head of the Kehillah, Marshall bitterly complained:

Conditions here are entirely unlike those amid which they [the immigrant leaders of Orthodox Judaism] were brought up. They cannot maintain their hold upon the young by their methods. They become mere objects of derision.

Unity

Many immigrants on the Lower East Side resented the much-needed financial aid offered by the wealthy "uptowners." In working toward a *kehillah* model of unifying all Jews, Rabbi Judah Magnes wrote an appeal to the Yiddish newspaper *Tageblatt* on September 29, 1909:

"It is time that our institutions be of our masses, and not above them. It is time that we work with the people rather than for the people."

The Murder That Shocked a Community

The death of "Beansey" Rosenthal in July 1912 sent shock waves through New York's Jewish community. Except for family and friends, his death was not so much mourned as regretted. He was neither a respected statesman nor an educator, not a scholar or religious leader. Herman "Beansey" Rosenthal was a common criminal, a gambler. Other Jewish criminals shot him to death. His murder was notable because it thrust the crime problems of the immigrant Jewish community directly into the glare of newspaper headlines.

During the sensational court trials, which ended with trips to the electric chair for Rosenthal's killers, millions read every new sordid newspaper story of police corruption and murder. Prominently featured in the stories were Jewish gangsters from the Lower East Side. The misdeeds of "Lefty Louie" and "Gyp the Blood" may have fascinated the average newspaper reader, but they were sources of extreme humiliation for many Jews.

The Kehillah appointed a determined detective, Abraham Shoenfeld, to investigate Jewish crime in the Lower East Side as a result of the "Beansey" Rosenthal murder. It was a clear signal that the Jews were finally prepared to "put their own house in order" and stop negative activity that could be used against their community. Shoenfeld's knowledge of New York's criminal world helped him establish a tireless group of agents and informers. They infiltrated criminal hideouts throughout the Lower East Side in order to identify known criminals and their associates. In favorite underworld gathering spots like Dora Gelb's candy store on First Street and Gluckner's Odessa Tea House on Tremont Street, Shoenfeld's agents gathered useful information for the police and the Kehillah. In time, criminal activity in the Lower East Side decreased along with the negative publicity.

Judah Magnes understood the challenges. "We seem to be a community of over a million souls, the largest Jewish community in the world, but we are hardly cognizant of what we possess or what we require."[2] He looked to the Kehillah to "wipe out invidious distinctions between East European, foreigner and native, 'uptown' Jew and 'downtown' Jew, rich and poor, and it will make us realize that the Jews are one people with a common history and with common hopes."[3]

"The Jews of New York," Magnes told the 1909 convention that met to create the Kehillah, "have a twofold problem . . . our relationship with [the] outside community . . . [and] internal problems. . . ."[4] The Kehillah conceived a Bureau of Social Morals to fight crime in the Lower East Side because it was deeply concerned about the image of the Jewish community created by the criminal acts of a few. Leaders of the Kehillah were quick to publicly issue a statement to defuse the idea that the Jewish community condoned criminal behavior:

As citizens of the city and as Jews, we view with profound indignation the profanation of the Jewish name brought about by these events, and the implication of Jews in practices of vices which have, up to very recent years, been proverbially unknown among our people.

Organizing to Serve

Duplication of existing services led to overlapping programs and inefficient use of funds. The Kehillah brought order out of chaos by organizing separate bureaus dealing with education, philanthropy, industry, employment, religion and social morals. By 1915, there were well over 3,500 separate Jewish institutions in New York. Although only a small number of them affiliated with the Kehillah, the Kehillah quickly became known as the most important and influential agency of the Jewish community, involving itself in a wide variety of community activities.

The Kehillah worked in diverse ways to improve the lives of Jews in New York. It tried to persuade newspapers to stop running employment ads specifying "Christians only need apply." At a time when theatres featured entertainers who stereotyped Jews in the worst possible manner, the Kehillah fought to remove these acts from the stage. As the number of homeless and orphaned Jewish children grew, the Kehillah established and funded institutions to care for them.

The Kehillah was concerned with the large number of labor strikes that pitted Jewish workers against Jewish factory owners. Through its Bureau of Industry, mediation and conciliation programs averted potential strikes and was able to obtain fair contracts for workers.

Perhaps the most successful of all the Kehillah activities were those concerned with Jewish education. The innovations pioneered by the Kehillah set up training facilities for teachers, established model schools and created modern textbooks and teaching materials. Its Bureau of Jewish Education succeeded in adapting American teaching practices to the needs of religious education.

Another legacy of the Kehillah was a workable system of raising money from the community to support the community. Rabbi Magnes may have been overoptimistic when he said, "we may eventually devise some means of collecting a per capita tax from the whole Jewish population to meet the needs of our charitable organizations."[6] The overlap of functions was deeply felt

King of the Gangsters

Unlike many of his gangster associates, Meyer Lansky lived a long, quiet life. He was credited with being the "brains" behind organized crime in America during the 1930s, 40s and 50s.

The character of Hyman Roth in the film *The Godfather* was modeled after Lansky, who is said to have boasted to his mob associates, "We're bigger than US Steel!"

by the small number of wealthy "uptown" Jews who were constantly asked for financial support. Louis Marshall told the Kehillah convention of 1914 ". . . some of us are being broken under the ever-increasing burden. It is time to call a halt or else the entire charitable system of New York City will go bankrupt. . . ."

A few years earlier, Judah Magnes said:

The Jews of New York City are highly organized if we consider their numerous and finely endowed philanthropic institutions. When some day a federation of these institutions is brought about, that will be another permanent basis for the organization of the Jews of the city. . . .

The Kehillah, according to Cyrus Sulzberger, one of its leaders, did bring together a cross section of New York Jews. "Rich men and men practically penniless; extreme socialists and extreme conservatives gather together and under parliamentary methods discuss the subjects they have in common."[7]

To Improve the Quality of Jewish Life

The United Jewish Communities is an umbrella organization that represents 189 Jewish federations and 400 independent communities throughout North America. In communities large and small local federations raise over $2 billion a year to support Jewish learning, Israel and human services for the poor and the elderly.

"Our vision reflects a fundamental principle: Fidelity to our age-old traditions and teachings must permeate our care for our people—including the poor, the troubled and disabled, the very young and very old. These values drive our desire to educate our youth, to hold sacred our traditions, and to build, with Israelis, a unified Jewish people." (From the mission statement of the United Jewish Communities)

Ultimately, the Kehillah experiment fell apart. With the outbreak of World War I, the attention of many immigrants turned to the needs of their devastated relatives in the "old country." Others decided that their reliance on the generosity of the wealthy "uptown" Jews hindered their own community development. The good intentions of the Kehillah were caught in the "crossfire of a struggle between a patrician Old Guard and a rising immigrant community."[8]

Rise of the Federations

Leaders of the Kehillah realized that solving the social and economic problems of the new immigrants required a more systematic and democratic way of raising and allocating money. The selfless philanthropy of the few wealthy Jews needed to evolve into a broad-based community federation system involving larger segments of the total Jewish community. The model for this already existed: The first Jewish federations were organized in Boston and Cincinnati late in the nineteenth century and in Cleveland in 1903. Other cities soon followed. In 1917, the Federation for the Support of Jewish Philanthropic Societies of New York was formed.

The federation, as a combination of agencies and contributors, could do what no single agency could do: it could jointly examine the requirements and assess the services of all the participating agencies and assign the funds where the needs were most urgent and where the greatest impact could be made.[9]

This poster of the Jewish Welfare Board encouraged all American Jews to support Jewish soldiers during World War I. The Yiddish caption reads, "We have built a home for them." *(National Archives)*

The first Passover seder dinner given by the Jewish Welfare Board for Jewish soldiers during World War I in Paris. The Jewish Welfare Board was founded during World War I to serve the special needs of American Jewish soldiers. *(National Archives)*

Early federation leaders developed unique fundraising methods that relied on personal solicitation by friends and business colleagues. These initial methods worked so well they are still in use today.

The successful fund-raising made it possible for federations to begin planning for the local needs of their respective communities. Within decades, federations became the local "addresses" for their respective Jewish

communities. They worked with national and international organizations before, during and after the Holocaust years to save Jewish lives and resettle survivors. They organized American Jewish financial support for the fledgling State of Israel. During the Six-Day War of June 1967, when the future of the State of Israel itself was in doubt, federations coordinated a massive fund-raising effort.

In 1939, the total amount raised by American Jewish federations was $40 million. By the early 1990s, that figure jumped to over $800 million. Until recently, close to 50 percent of that money went to Israel. With peace efforts between Israel and its Arab neighbors well underway in the 1980s and 1990s and Israel's economy taking off, federations refocused their efforts inward. The original Kehillah concerns with local Jewish community problems came full circle: from immigration, crime, anti-Semitism and poverty to intermarriage, education and Jewish cultural continuity.

Jewish activism in the 1960s and 70s led to the freeing of Jews from the Soviet Union. For decades after World War II, anti-Semitism was alive and well in the Soviet Union. Jews mobilized to urge the United States to intervene and save Soviet Jews. Their lobbying and political activism resulted in large-scale emigration of Soviet Jews to Israel and the United States. (*Rauh Archives, Historical Society of Western Pennsylvania*)

CHAPTER 4

Fighting Bigotry: The Lynching of Leo Frank

"We are Americans, first, last and all the time. Nothing else that we are by faith or race or fate qualifies our Americanism."

RABBI STEPHEN S. WISE

P olice Commissioner Bingham's harsh words against the Jewish residents of New York's Lower East Side in 1908 enraged the city's Jews and led to the creation of the Kehillah. But this was not the first time the Jews confronted bigotry in America. Governor Peter Stuyvesant greeted the very first Jewish settlers in New Amsterdam in 1654 with intolerance. "To give liberty to the Jews will be very detrimental," he said. Setting a model for other groups, the Jews actively and successfully fought every discriminatory obstacle placed before them. This instance was just the first in a series of continuing battles for equality for themselves and others.

Hatred of Jews was a legacy of European anti-Semitism. Over centuries, the Jews had largely become a people apart, living in a Christian world, and religious intolerance led to discrimination. In the New World, Jews faced legal attempts by others to restrict their rights. "Many colonies did not make Jews welcome.

Jews faced residency bans, restrictions on businesses, home ownership and citizenship."[1]

With the passage of time, they gradually gained acceptance and recognition as full and equal citizens of the United States. Yet, despite these legal guarantees, anti-Semitism was never far removed from the daily lives of American Jews. By the 1870s, the children of German Jewish immigrants had become successful in business, medicine, law and teaching. "As they became more conspicuous in society, others began to view them as social and economic threats. The result was a period of unprecedented anti-Semitism in America."[2]

In 1877, Joseph Seligman, one of the wealthiest men in the United States, brought his family to Saratoga

Echoes of Hatred

While discrimination and exclusion were serious acts of bigotry, they paled in comparison to events in Europe. In 1894, a Jewish officer in the French army, Captain Alfred Dreyfus, was accused of treason. For the next twelve years, France and the world were obsessed by the Dreyfus affair. From the beginning, rampant anti-Semitism clouded reason. Even after proof of Dreyfus's innocence emerged, many continued to believe him guilty simply because he was Jewish.

In 1903, a particularly violent attack on Jews occurred in the Russian city of Kishinev. Nearly fifty Jewish men, women and children were killed and thousands more raped and injured. The civilized world was shocked and universally condemned the Russians. Attacks on Jews were frequent in Russia but none attracted as much worldwide attention as the one in Kishinev. Attention to the massacre could perhaps be attributed to the fact that international communications had improved, or it might have been that people were growing more sensitive to public discrimination. Despite the outrage, the old prejudices continued.

In 1911, a Jew, Mendel Beilis, was falsely accused of ritual murder in the death of a young Russian boy. When the case came to trial two years later, a Russian jury unexpectedly declared Beilis not guilty. The verdict came as a relief but could not diminish anti-Jewish sentiment in Russia and elsewhere.

Springs, New York, for an annual summer vacation at the Grand Union Hotel. To his surprise and embarrassment, he was turned away. The new owners of the hotel had issued an order that "no Israelite shall be permitted in the future to stop at the hotel." The next day, a front-page headline in *The New York Times* reporting the incident proclaimed, "Outrage in Saratoga." While politicians and clergy denounced this public act of discrimination, Jews soon found themselves barred from major industries, hotels, social clubs and private schools. Famous universities including Harvard and Columbia instituted quotas limiting the number of Jewish students. Restrictive clauses in legal contracts prevented Jews from buying or renting apartments or homes in desirable sections of American cities.

Jews in small numbers had been among the original settlers of the southern United States. A few had even risen to positions of political and economic power. During the Civil War, Jewish soldiers fought and died on both sides. A Jew, Judah Benjamin, was secretary of state in the Confederate government. Although the war ended in 1865, bitterness and distrust of strangers lingered well into the twentieth century.

By 1913, the largest Jewish population in the South was concentrated in Atlanta, Georgia. There, 3,500 Jews lived quiet but generally comfortable lives surrounded by largely poor, undereducated rural neighbors who vented their frustrations on "Northerners," "Yankees," and "rich Jews."

Murder at the Pencil Factory

That year, on Saturday, April 26, the city prepared to celebrate Confederate Memorial Day with a massive parade. Thirteen-year-old Mary Phagan, dressed in her finest dress and carrying a pink parasol, left her modest home to join the happy throngs lining Peachtree Street. On her way, she stopped at the nearly empty National Pencil Company factory to pick up back wages that were due her. Like many other rural Georgians transplanted to the big city, school was out of the question; Mary had to work to insure her family's survival. Her job with the pencil company was to fasten rubber tips on the pencils. She worked ten hours a day for twelve cents an hour.

Newt Lee, the African-American night watchman, found the body of Mary Phagan in the pencil company's basement early the next morning. She had been strangled to death. Coming on the heels of a number of unsolved murders of girls and women in the area, news of Mary's murder quickly spread. Several company employees were initially arrested and held for investigation before suspicion finally rested upon the last person who admitted seeing Mary Phagan alive, Leo Frank.

Frank was twenty-nine years old, raised in Brooklyn, New York, and a graduate of Cornell University. He moved to Atlanta in 1908 to supervise the National Pencil Company factory. He quickly became an active member of Atlanta's Jewish community, married a local Jewish girl, and, in 1913, was elected president of the Atlanta chapter of B'nai B'rith, the national Jewish fraternal organization.

The police investigation uncovered a number of unsubstantiated rumors and conflicting witness testimonies, but this did not prevent a grand jury from handing down an indictment for murder against Leo Frank. From the beginning, the issue of Frank's religion was never far from the surface. One newspaper stated, "Our little girl—ours by the eternal God!—has been pursued to a hideous death by this filthy perverted Jew from New York."[3]

Two barely literate notes found near Mary Phagan's body puzzled the police. They seemed to accuse the watchman Newt Lee of the murder. When James Conley, an African-American sweeper at the factory was found rinsing a bloody shirt, he too was arrested. Under questioning, Conley admitted to writing the notes. He first said that Leo Frank asked him to write them the day *before* the murder. A few days later Conley changed his story and claimed that Frank ordered him to write them *after* the murder. Conley also volunteered that Frank asked him to watch the stairway leading to the office, and while there he had fallen asleep. The sweeper told police that a sharp whistle coming from Frank's office awakened him. When he entered the room, Conley claimed to have found Frank shaking and nervous. According to Conley, Frank then told him to write the notes and muttered, "Why should I hang?" Conley's story appeared flawed and contradictory, but this did not stop the police from pursuing Frank as the main suspect.

Assigning Guilt

Although Newt Lee, the watchman who found the body, was considered a prime suspect, he was quickly overlooked in favor of Frank. Decades later an African-American preacher wrote about Lee: " . . . this one old Negro would be poor atonement for the life of this innocent girl. But when on the next day the police arrested a Jew, and a Yankee Jew at that, all of the inborn prejudice against Jews rose up in a feeling of satisfaction, that here would be a victim worthy to pay for the crime."[4]

Trial by Jury

The murder trial of Leo Frank began on July 28, 1913. It was a summer of high temperatures and high emotions in Atlanta. People sat listlessly inside the courtroom as crowds outside strained to hear snatches of testimony through the open windows. Chants of "Hang the Jew!" and the inflammatory words of traveling preachers—"The Jew is the synagogue of Satan!"[5]—nearly drowned out the legal proceedings inside. Hawkers on the street sold a variety of anti-Semitic pamphlets.

The testimony of witnesses—much of which was later recanted—proved damaging to Frank. One woman, the owner of a "house of ill-repute," testified that Leo Frank was a frequent visitor. She told the court that on the evening of the murder Frank had called to request a room for himself and a young girl. She claimed that

Power of the Press

The anti-Jewish, anti-Frank hatred was fanned in large measure by the writings of Thomas E. Watson, a former member of Congress and presidential candidate of the Populist Party. Through his popular newspaper, *The Jeffersonian*, Watson maintained a steady shrill and abusive tirade against Jews, Catholics and "outsiders." The Frank case provided him with endless opportunities to promote his feelings against "the filthy, perverted Jew of New York." "Frank belonged to the Jewish aristocracy, and it was determined by the rich Jews that no aristocrat of their race should die for the death of a working-class gentile," he wrote. "The next Leo Frank case in Georgia will never reach the courthouse," Watson warned.

The lynching of Leo Frank. The murder of Leo Frank galvanized the American Jewish community to action against discrimination and bigotry. All Jews, whether recent immigrants or long-time citizens, felt personally vulnerable to acts of hatred. (*American Jewish Archives, Hebrew Union College*)

Frank told her, "It's a matter of life and death." Mr. Watson seized on that testimony to brand Frank a pervert who routinely arranged sexual orgies in the pencil company office.

Another woman testified that she saw Frank walking down the street with James Conley. "How did you know it was Frank?" the prosecutor asked. "Because," the witness answered, "as they walked along he had his face very close to the Negro, and that's how I knew he was a Jew."[6] James Conley provided further fuel for the fire. He testified that he frequently served as a "lookout" for his boss when Frank entertained young women in his office. But no women were ever found who could verify that story.

Conley told the court that on the day of the murder he had helped Frank drag Mary Phagan's body into the elevator and down to the basement. Although none of the lawyers picked up on it at the trial, it was later proven that the elevator had not been used that day. Conley also testified that Frank offered him money if he "kept his mouth shut." When it was his turn to testify, Leo Frank forcefully denied Conley's accusations.

In all, over three hundred witnesses testified during the twenty-five day trial. In closing arguments, lawyers for Leo Frank told the jury that no evidence existed to prove the guilt of their client. One of them argued that "if Frank hadn't been a Jew, there would never have been any prosecution against him." Furthermore, they stated that the guilty person was none other than the prosecution's star witness, James Conley. The prosecutor, Hugh Dorsey, tried to downplay the aura of anti-Semitism that surrounded the trial. "The word 'Jew' never escaped our lips," he said. He then mentioned the names of well-known Jewish criminals. The Jews, he reasoned, "rise to heights sublime, but they also sink to the lowest depths of degradation!"[7] In the end, it was Conley's word against Frank's.

In an unusual act, the judge, fearing violence, requested that the defendant be kept away from the courtroom when the case went to the jury. Frank's lawyers agreed. On Monday, August 25, the jury took less than four hours to find Leo Frank guilty of murder. It was the first time that the testimony of an African-American was used to convict a white person in a Southern court.

Atlantans were jubilant. As National Guard troops took up positions around the city, people in the streets and stores clapped and cheered while others danced happily in front of the pencil company building. "The very atmosphere of the courtroom was charged with an electric current of indignation . . . the courtroom and streets were filled with an angry, determined crowd, ready to seize the defendant if the jury had found him not guilty," reported the *Atlanta Journal.*[8]

On Tuesday morning, Leo Frank stood before the judge. When asked if he had anything to say before sen-

The Ballad of Mary Phagan

The jury in Leo Frank's trial took less than four hours to reach a guilty verdict. Outside the courthouse a mob danced with joy. On the courthouse steps Fiddlin' John Carson sang "The Ballad of Mary Phagan" to a receptive crowd. The song became an instant hit throughout the South.

Little Mary Phagan
She went to town one day;
She went to the pencil factory
To get her weekly pay . . .

Leo Frank he met her
With a brutish heart and grin;
He says to little Mary,
"You'll never see home again."

She fell down on her knees
To Leo Frank and pled.
He picked up a plank from
the trash pile
And beat her o'er the head . . .

Judge Roan passed the sentence;
He passed it very well;
The Christian doers of heaven
Sent Leo Frank to hell . . .[9]

tencing, Frank answered simply, "I am innocent. Further than that, I will state that my case is in the hands of my counsel." The judge then sentenced Frank to "be hanged by the neck until he is dead." A few months later, the same judge sentenced James Conley to serve a year on a chain gang for being an accessory to the murder.

An editorial in the *Macon (Georgia) Daily Telegraph* stated, ". . . the long case and its bitterness has hurt the city greatly in that it has opened a seemingly impassable chasm between the people of the Jewish race and the gentiles. . . ."[10]

Reaction outside of Georgia was more sympathetic to Frank. Newspapers called for a new trial. "Justice Demands a New Trial for Frank," blared a headline in the *Baltimore Sun*. As Leo Frank's lawyers began a series of appeals to higher courts, some prominent Southern Jews appealed to Jews in the North for support and advice. Many Jews throughout the country were concerned that the conviction of Frank, coming so soon after the Dreyfus affair in France and the Beilis trial in Russia in 1913, would lead to widespread discrimination against Jews.

Indeed, the American Jewish Committee, originally founded to counteract anti-Semitism in Russia, quickly entered the fight to overturn Frank's conviction. One of the organization's founders, Adolph Ochs, publisher of *The New York Times*, increased coverage of Frank's case in his newspaper. These efforts succeeded only in increasing Southern resentment of Northerners.

The Governor Intercedes

One legal defeat followed another as the appeals continued. With the last appeal denied, and an execution date set for June 22, 1915, the case reached the governor. Only he could prevent the execution of Leo Frank. John M. Slaton was nearing the end of his term of office. Pressure on him to carry out the execution mounted throughout the state, led by Thomas Watson and *The Jeffersonian*. One letter to the editor threatened, "If the big Jew editors, bankers and others don't look out they will fan into flame the smoldering embers of that old ground-in-the-bone prejudice."

On June 12, a huge mass meeting was held on the grounds of the state capital urging the governor not to accede to the demands of "Yankee Jews" and prevent the hanging. The governor reviewed the trial material carefully, including letters from the original judge and the prosecutor's law partner that stated doubt of Frank's guilt. Early on the morning of June 21, 1915, his next to last day in office, a weary Governor Slaton entered his bedroom and informed his wife, "It may mean my death or worse, but I have ordered the sentence commuted." Mrs. Slaton kissed her husband and said, "I would rather be the widow of a brave and honorable man than the wife of a coward."[11]

The governor had not pardoned Frank. He had only changed the sentence from death to life imprisonment. "I would be a murderer if I allowed that man to hang," he wrote in his commutation decision. The governor secretly ordered Frank to be moved from Atlanta to the state penitentiary in Milledgeville. Supporters of Leo Frank were relieved at the governor's decision to commute the sentence. Opponents were angered beyond words. Armed mobs convened on the governor's mansion. They broke windows and threw rocks at the troops guarding the governor. Throughout Georgia, the governor was hanged in effigy and Jews were threatened. One sign in Marietta read, "John M. Slaton, King of the Jews and Georgia's Traitor Forever." A vigilance committee in the same city distributed flyers to Jewish shopkeepers declaring, "We mean to rid Marietta of all Jews . . . you can heed this warning or stand the punishment the committee may see fit to deal out to you."

Thomas Watson urged Georgians to take the law into their own hands and hang Frank themselves. "We will make certain that no other Georgia girl . . . will die a horrible death defending her virtue against a rich, depraved Sodomite Jew." At the June 26 inauguration of his successor, Governor Slaton was heavily guarded. Immediately after the ceremony, he took his wife on an extended vacation out of state. In New York, he told reporters, "I did what I thought was right. Conley had the same opportunity and much more disposition to assault and murder Mary Phagan." Slaton's political life was over.

A Southern Lynching

O n July 18, a fellow prisoner attacked Leo Frank with a butcher knife and nearly killed him by cutting his throat. Less than a month later on the night of August 16, 1915, a raiding party of twenty-five masked men calling themselves The Knights of Mary Phagan entered the prison. They quickly handcuffed the warden, overpowered the guards and cut the telephone lines. They removed Leo Frank from his hospital room and forced him into one of the eight automobiles waiting outside. "You will find him on Mary Phagan's grave," one of the masked men told a guard.

Early in the morning of August 17, the caravan arrived in Marietta. There in a grove they led Frank to a large oak tree and revealed a hangman's rope. "Mr. Frank," the group's leader said, "we are now going to do what the law said to do, hang you by the neck until you are dead." Frank appeared calm and made only one request. He asked that his wedding ring be given to his wife. The men threw the rope over a heavy branch, put a blindfold over his eyes and the noose around his neck. Then, they lifted him onto a crudely planked table and kicked it away. Within moments, Leo Frank was dead.

A crowd of onlookers quickly gathered to watch as Frank's body twisted in the wind for two hours. Some people took photographs of the body while others cut pieces of his nightshirt or the hanging rope as souvenirs. "There's life in the old land yet," a gleeful Thomas Watson later wrote. The men who lynched Leo Frank were well known in Marietta, but no one was ever charged with his murder.

Reaction to the lynching came from around the world. "The State of Georgia cannot remove this blot of shame," wrote *The New York Times*. In response, the *Macon (Georgia) Daily Telegraph*, wrote, "The men who lynched Leo Frank went ahead with clear consciences. It would never have happened had the rest of the nation left this state to mind its own business."

Thomas Watson wrote in *The Jeffersonian*, "A Vigilance Committee redeems Georgia and carries out the sentence of the law on the Jew who raped and murdered the little Gentile girl, Mary Phagan . . . In putting the murderer to death the Vigilance Committee has done what the Sheriff would have done if Slaton had not been of the same mold as Benedict Arnold. Let Jew libertines take notice. Georgia is not for sale to rich criminals."

The Truth at Last

For decades, the murder of Mary Phagan remained one of this country's most debated historical events. The case came to a dramatic end in 1982, decades after the lynching of Leo Frank. That year, Alonzo Mann, close to death, made a startling videotaped confession. As a fourteen-year-old office boy at the National Pencil Company in 1913, he witnessed James Conley carrying the body of Mary Phagan to the steps leading to the building's basement. Conley warned the young boy not to get involved. "If you mention this, I'll kill you," he had warned the boy. Alonzo was frightened and kept silent throughout the trial.

In 1982, reporters for a Tennessee newspaper uncovered his story. A lie detector test confirmed the truth of his allegation. "I believe in the sight of God," Mann said, "that Jim Conley killed Mary Phagan to get her money to buy beer. Leo Frank was innocent." In 1983, the Georgia Board of Pardons and Paroles denied a request for a pardon. They claimed that Alonzo Mann's revelation only incriminated James Conley but did not prove Leo Frank's innocence. Finally, in 1986, the Board reversed itself and granted the pardon.

Standing Up to Bigotry

Even as Jews were being assimilated into American life, the dread of anti-Semitism was never distant. The Frank case had a profound effect on the American Jewish community. In 1913, in response to that tragedy, members of B'nai B'rith founded the Anti-Defamation League. The charter stated that the organization existed "to stop the defamation of the Jewish people . . . to secure justice and fair treatment for all citizens alike . . . to put an end forever to unjust and unfair treatment for all citizens alike . . . to put an end forever to unjust and unfair discrimination against, and ridicule of, any sect or body of citizens."

Since its founding, the ADL has led the fight against discrimination and intolerance of all people. Working with lawmakers and law enforcement officials, the ADL helps enact laws that target hateful acts against minorities. It keeps a watchful eye on hate groups and promotes a variety of programs that help people confront prejudice and create understanding among the diverse groups that make up the United States.

We tend to associate anti-Semitism in the 1920s and 1930s with Germany and the rise of Nazism. Yet during that period the voices of hatred were not silent in the United States either. Among the shrillest purveyors of anti-Jewish propaganda were some famous Americans. Most notable among them was the industrialist Henry Ford. Through his widely distributed newspaper, the *Dearborn Independent*, Ford published a continuing series of articles attacking Jews, their patriotism and character. As proof, he reprinted the *Protocols of the*

An act of hatred in the 1930s. Even as the Nazis were rising to power in Germany, acts of anti-Semitism continued in the United States. (YIVO Institute)

Elders of Zion, a forged document from czarist Russia that "proved" the existence of a secret international Jewish plot to control the world.

He constantly accused the New York Kehillah, the Anti-Defamation League of B'nai B'rith, and the American Jewish Committee of plotting to "Judaize" American society:

> *The Jews' determination to wipe out of public life every sign of the predominant Christian character of the United States, is the only active form of religious intolerance in the country today . . . Not content with the fullest liberty to follow their own faith in peace and quietness, in a country where none dares make them afraid, the Jews declare . . . that every sight and sound of anything Christian is an invasion of their peace and quietness, and so they stamp it out wherever they can reach it through political means.[12]*

Although divisions within the Kehillah ultimately led to the organization's end, Ford accused it of controlling the American Jewish community: "The New York Kehillah is the largest and most powerful union of Jews in the world. The center of Jewish world power has been transferred to that city. That is the meaning of the heavy migration of Jews all over the world toward New York."

A key target of Ford's hatred was Louis Marshall, who was perhaps the most prominent Jewish spokesperson of the time and the head of the American Jewish Committee. In his newspaper, Ford commented, "It would be interesting to know how the name of 'Marshall' found its way to the Jewish gentleman. It is not a common name, even among Jews who change their names."[13] Referring to the involvement of Marshall in the case of Leo Frank, Ford wrote, "It seems to be a part of

Hammerin' Hank

American Jews in the 1930s and 40s faced physical danger and blatant discrimination in schools and places of employment. Even the famous were not immune. Hank Greenberg, the son of Jewish immigrants, was one of the best-known sports figures of the 1930s. As a hero of the Detroit Tigers who was later elected to the Baseball Hall of Fame, Greenberg frequently faced anti-Semitic slurs from fellow players and fans. Once, fans even threw pork chops at him while he was on the field. Yet he endured this show of hatred to become a baseball hero—"Hammerin' Hank." His success was a source of pride for the Jewish community.

When he chose to attend Yom Kippur services rather than play in a crucial game, his decision was received with respect by most Americans and with immense pride by other Jews. Hank Greenberg's behavior on and off the field inspired Jackie Robinson, the first African-American player in major-league baseball. Robinson later remarked that Hank Greenberg's example gave him "the strength and endurance to just keep on playing, in spite of prejudice and discrimination."

Jewish loyalty to prevent if possible the Gentile law being enforced against Jews . . . the Dreyfus case and the Frank case are examples of the endless publicity the Jews secure in behalf of their own people."

Ford wrote against the ADL's successful fight against the common newspaper practice of the time—to identify Jewish individuals, often those accused of crimes, by their religion. "For this state of affairs," Ford wrote, "the Anti-Defamation League receives the credit . . . it has concealed the Jew where he wishes to be concealed. . . ."[14]

Even the successes in eliminating discrimination met with mockery from Ford:

Louis Marshall is leader of that movement that will force the Jew by law into places where he is not wanted. The law, compelling hotel keepers to permit Jews to make their hotels a place of resort if they want to, has been steadily pushed. Such a law is practically a Bolshevik order to destroy property, for it is commonly known what Jewish patronage does to public places.[15]

Public Hatred, Private Suffering

Henry Ford's anti-Semitic crusade had a receptive audience in the United States. The time between the two world wars was a period of uncertainty and fear. Suspicion of foreigners led to the enactment of strict immigration laws in 1924. Jews reacted reflexively by shrinking from the public limelight. They invoked what many called "the shasha syndrome"—don't call attention to yourself.

After the presidential election of 1936, the *B'nai B'rith Magazine* reported: "During the election campaign just over we heard a great deal to this effect: that the Jew effaces himself as much as possible from public life lest he appear too prominent and make himself a shining mark for ene-

---

The Words That Brought Down a Hero

Excerpts from Charles A. Lindbergh's September 11, 1941, speech in Des Moines, Iowa:

"The three most important groups who have been pressing this country toward war are the British, the Jewish and the Roosevelt administration."

"Instead of agitating for war, the Jewish groups in this country should be opposing it in every possible way for they will be among the first to feel its consequences."

"Their [the Jews] greatest danger to this country lies in their large ownership and influence in our motion pictures, our press, our radio and our government."

An outdoor suburban pool of the Jewish Community Center of Pittsburgh, 1969. As Jewish communities moved from the cities into suburbia, they built synagogues, Jewish community centers and recreational facilities that mirrored their new prosperity and place in American society. *(Rauh Archives, Historical Society of Western Pennsylvania)*

mies." But this did not deter others from pursuing anti-Jewish activities.

Radio provided anti-Semites with a national audience. Father Charles Coughlin, a Catholic priest who hosted a radio program, spewed hate for Jews and justified the rise of Nazism in Germany as a "defense reaction" against Jewish power. Famous aviator Charles A. Lindbergh publicly praised Nazism and accused Jews of conspiring to bring America into a war against Germany.

The Decline of Overt Anti-Semitism

There was a marked decline in overt anti-Semitism in the years following World War II, as the American Jewish community became increasingly more self-confident. Violence gave way to more subtle forms of discrimination. The Academy Award-winning film *Gentleman's Agreement* (1947) gave theatergoers a glimpse into the world of bigotry and hatred.

Federal and state laws enacted in the last half of the twentieth century virtually eliminated outright discrimination against all minorities. Nonetheless, anti-Semitism remained a part of American life. Instead of blatant hotel

In the midst of the United States' civil rights struggle, Jews were not immune from physical attack. On October 13, 1958, a dynamite explosion in Atlanta, Georgia, heavily damaged a Reform temple. (*Associated Press*)

and employment advertisements barring Jews, bigotry adopted a less visible face.

Today, one can find anti-Semitic views primarily in the literature of hate groups or on Internet websites but rarely on commercial radio and television stations or in mainstream newspapers. In his biography, *My Awakening*, Ku Klux Klan leader David Duke wrote, "No one has to tell Jews to destroy gentile pride, heritage, honor, loyalty, tradition, while at the same time building up their own. It is in their programming." In an interview, he said, "The Jews are trying to destroy all other cultures . . . as a survival mechanism . . . the only Nazi country in the world is Israel."[16]

Overall, the Anti-Defamation League has documented a decline in the number of Americans who hold anti-Jewish views. A recent ADL survey discovered that 12 percent of Americans harbor anti-Semitic opinions. This figure is down from 29 percent in 1964. Even as hardcore anti-Semitism has declined, right-wing fringe groups such as Aryan Nations, National Alliance and "skinheads" remain dangerously in the background. While most Americans decry threats of violence against Jews, occasional acts of violence and graffiti continue to remind everyone that hate still exists.

The ADL, founded in response to the Leo Frank case, continues to monitor hate-group activities throughout the country. Dory Schary, a playwright, Hollywood producer and long time national chairperson of the ADL, said, "The trial of Leo Frank had a galvanic effect on the men who created the League . . . the story

Old Hatred: New Technology

The Internet has provided hate groups with a new vehicle for disseminating their ideas. With a click, today's bigot can instantly send hate messages to thousands of people at the same time. The Internet has given new life to some old anti-Semitic literature such as Henry Ford's four-volume work *The International Jew* first published in 1920. Likewise, many of Ford's anti-Semitic articles from the *Dearborn Independent* have resurfaced on the Net.

President Dwight D. Eisenhower addressing the fortieth anniversary dinner of the Anti-Defamation League of B'nai B'rith. Presidents in the twentieth century, regardless of political party, have been frequent guests at major meetings of Jewish American organizations. (Dwight D. Eisenhower Library)

of Leo Frank struck the American Jewish community like nothing before in its experience."[17]

Today, through such programs as A World of Difference, the ADL has been responsible for instituting anti-hate curricula in public schools around the country. Abraham Foxman, the ADL's national director, said:

We have a responsibility to remember the hideous truth that no one is safe from the madness of intolerance. We have a responsibility not to remain silent when any group is maligned or talked about or treated with contempt . . . no matter who the victim is or who is the perpetrator.

CHAPTER 5

Creating
American Culture:
The Jazz Singer,
Gershwin and Greenberg

Eddie Cantor was not the only Jew to leave the Lower East Side for the stage and screen. George Jessel, Fanny Brice, George Burns and Sophie Tucker made their way up the entertainment ladder from the Yiddish theater to vaudeville and then to radio, television and film. Other children of Jewish immigrants took their talents in different directions, and in their own way significantly influenced American popular culture as well.

Artists such as Chaim Gross and Roy Lichtenstein redefined American art. Writers like Saul Bellow, Susan Sontag and Philip Roth helped to shape the modern American novel. And everywhere, people then and now hum popular American tunes written by Jewish songwriters. They were created by Jewish composers such as Irving Berlin ("God Bless America," "White Christmas,") and George Gershwin ("Rhapsody in Blue," "Fascinating Rhythm"). Jerome Kern once said, "Irving Berlin has no place in American music. He *is* American music."[1]

Al Jolson: The Jazz Singer

No entertainer symbolized the rapid upward movement of Jews into American mainstream more than Al Jolson. Born Asa Yoelson in Lithuania, he grew up in Washington, D.C., the son of a cantor. As with many children of immigrants, the lure of American culture won out over the traditional Jewish life rooted in Eastern Europe. Al started in vaudeville, and quickly became a show business phenomenon. He and his distinctive voice were already familiar to many Americans when he starred in *The Jazz Singer*, the movie that marked the emergence of Jews into mainstream American consciousness. This movie not only revolutionized film history, it also made public the growing rift between young American Jews and their European-born parents.

The Flight of Charles A. Levine

All eyes were on Roosevelt Field in New York as three teams of daring aviators competed to be the first to fly the Atlantic. Charles A. Lindbergh was, of course, first and won the accolades of the American public.

The second plane to fly across three weeks later was the *Columbia*, flown by Clarence Chamberlain and the plane's owner, Charles A. Levine. The plane, landing deep in Germany, actually flew farther than Lindbergh's *Spirit of St. Louis*, which landed in Paris. Millions followed the journey of the *Columbia*, and Levine's name appeared in newspaper headlines across America. On Broadway, one of the most popular songs in 1927 was "Levine and His Flying Machine." At a time when Jews rarely received positive publicity in the press, Levine was a hero and role model.

Jolson died in 1950, and in his eulogy, actor George Jessel explained the phenomenal impact that Jolson and other Jewish entertainers had on America:

In 1910, the Jewish people who emigrated from Europe to come here were a sad lot. Their humor came out of their own troubles . . . When they sang, they sang with lament in their hearts . . . And then there came [Jolson], vibrantly pulsing with life and courage . . . and told the world that the Jew in America did not only have to sing in sorrow but could shout happily . . . Jolson is the happiest portrait that can ever be painted about an American of the Jewish faith.[2]

Irving Berlin (left) and Eddie Cantor. Although raised in Yiddish-speaking homes on the Lower East Side, they both contributed greatly to American popular culture. Berlin wrote some of America's most widely known and beloved songs including "God Bless America." Cantor, who popularized many Berlin songs, was a favorite entertainer right into the 1950s. *(Special Collections Department, University Research Library, UCLA)*

Watching the 1927 version of *The Jazz Singer* may seem quaint and even foreign to today's moviegoers, but to those who viewed it when it was first released, it was fresh and revealing. *The Jazz Singer* was the first "talking picture." It was not much by today's standards, but in 1927 it was revolutionary. It won two Academy Awards and, more significantly, it signaled the end of the silent movie era. No more would theatergoers have to read dialogue flashed onto the movie screen. Instead, the voices of the actors were synchronized with their lips. The most remembered words uttered by Jolson in the film were also prophetic, "Wait a minute! Wait a minute! You ain't heard nuthin' yet."

In some ways, the technological achievement of the "talking picture" overshadowed a story line that in many ways described Jolson's own life. In *The Jazz Singer* Jakie Rabinowitz, son of a cantor, is torn between his father's desire for Jakie to follow in his footsteps as cantor and the lure of show business. Jewish immigrants watching the film not only marveled at the wizardry of sound, they were also filled with the excitement of seeing themselves and their struggle to become Americans depicted on

The Landing

Charles A. Levine and Clarence Chamberlin landed their plane, *The Columbia*, in Cottbus, Germany on June 6, 1927. Awaiting them was the town band, playing a near-passable version of the "The Star Spangled Banner." A handmade American flag with less than the required number of stars fluttered proudly. After several official speeches, during which Levine and Chamberlin were showered with gifts and mementos, they were made honorary citizens of Cottbus. The honor guaranteed them the lifetime privilege of living in the town free of charge. Both were invited to return in 1930 to help the town celebrate its thousandth birthday. Ironically, when the Nazis came to power in 1933, Levine's citizenship was unceremoniously withdrawn by the Cottbus town council since Levine was Jewish.

Charles A. Levine (third from left) and Clarence Chamberlin (second from right) in front of their airplane, *The Columbia*, after landing in Germany in 1927. The Jewish aviator, who was the second person to safely fly across the Atlantic, brought a sense of pride to American Jews at a time of mounting bigotry and anti-Semitism. *(National Air-Space Museum, Smithsonian Institution)*

screen. In a definitive moment, Jack tells his father, "You're of the Old World! If you were born here, you'd feel the same as I do—tradition is all right, but this is another day! I'll live my life as I see fit!"

America was not Europe. Although parents knew this, they found it difficult to abandon centuries-old traditions. But their children had no such attachments. They were growing up in a country with endless possibilities and they wanted to be part of the excitement. For them, the religious practices of their parents seemed a stumbling block to attaining the "American dream."

In the film Jakie Rabinowitz, torn between the old ways and Broadway, transforms himself into Jack Robin, a jazz singer. His father disowns him, but Jack keeps in contact with his mother. As years pass, Jack Robin becomes a successful entertainer. As his father lies dying,

83

Jack is called upon to take his father's place to sing the *Kol Nidrei* prayer on Yom Kippur. Coincidentally, the service is scheduled for the same time as Jack's opening on Broadway. What is he to do? Despite his aspirations, he cancels his opening and sings in the synagogue. He honors his father and his tradition this one time, but he does not give up his show business career to succeed his father as cantor. Jack Robin's action mirrored the "three-day-a-year" habit of many American Jews who went to synagogue only on important holidays such as Rosh Hashanah and Yom Kippur.

The Jazz Singer was the first major Hollywood film with a Jewish theme that was designed for a general audience. Along with popular songs such as "Mammy" and "Toot, Toot, Tootsie, Goodbye" Americans got to hear "Kol Nidrei." Famed Cantor Yossele Rosenblatt was a featured cast member, playing himself in the film. Before the advent of other mass media such as radio and television, *The Jazz Singer* introduced many Americans to a Jewish life they never knew existed. The poignant saga demonstrated that Jews, like other Americans, faced generational conflicts. For people who lived far

On the Air

Jewish comedians were the most popular performers on radio and television. Most of them learned their craft in vaudeville or in the "Borscht Belt" summer hotels in the Catskill Mountains of New York.

The most popular personality in the early years of television was Milton Berle. "Uncle Miltie" had a long career in vaudeville and radio before becoming television's first superstar, known as "Mr. Television." His brash and loud form of comedy bordered on rudeness and insult, but viewers loved it. Even though there was nothing outwardly Jewish about his performances, whenever he threw a Yiddish word or phrase into his frenetic comedy ("I'm schvitzing [sweating]." "My sheytel [wig] is falling.") Jews across America basked in their private glow of acceptance.

from the large cities of the East Coast and had never met a Jew and for those who harbored uninformed prejudices about them, the film demonstrated that Jews could still maintain spiritual ties to tradition while joining the American mainstream.

The "Invisible" Jews of Hollywood

The founders of the major Hollywood studios were Jewish, many of them born in Europe. They never attended film schools but gravitated to Hollywood when they found other business opportunities closed to them as Jews. Most downplayed their Jewish backgrounds in their private lives and also at the studios they ran. Yet in their own ways they transformed their Jewish backgrounds into films containing universal themes. An example is the film *They Won't Forget*, which was a fictional account of the Leo Frank case. In the film, Frank is not the Jewish factory manager, but a Yankee professor. The Jewish studio heads no doubt were troubled by the discrimination they faced, but it didn't stop them from having idealized views of their adopted country and through their filmmaking their affection for America helped to shape American's views of themselves. Historian Aljean Harmetz said, "I'm not sure there was an American Dream before Jews came to Hollywood."[3]

Anyone viewing *The Jazz Singer* today would consider the use of blackface by Al Jolson to be a racist act. But at the turn of the twentieth century, it was customary for many actors and actresses, Jewish and non-Jewish, to perform with faces darkened with burnt cork.

Selected Jewish Writer Award Winners

The National Book Award for Fiction

2000	Susan Sontag	In America
1995	Philip Roth	Sabbath's Theater
1986	E.L. Doctorow	World's Fair
1971	Saul Bellow	Mr. Sammler's Planet
1967	Bernard Malamud	The Fixer
1965	Saul Bellow	Herzog
1954	Saul Bellow	The Adventures of Augie March

The Pulitzer Prize for Fiction

2001	Michael Chabon	The Amazing Adventures of Kavalier and Clay
1988	Philip Roth	American Pastoral
1980	Norman Mailer	The Executioner's Song
1976	Saul Bellow	Humboldt's Gift
1967	Bernard Malamud	The Fixer
1952	Herman Wouk	The Caine Mutiny
1925	Edna Ferber	So Big

Minstrel shows featuring white people in blackface were also commonplace. One writer later explained, "In this very Jewish industry, they . . . thought that depicting Jews would promote anti-Semitism, so they hid it. Blackface is a metaphor for that."[4]

The Jazz Singer portrayed the dilemma of Jewish life in the United States in the 1920s. In the super-charged anti-Semitic years of the 1930s and early 1940s, Jewish film studio executives, like other American Jews, were nervous about calling attention to themselves. No other major films with Jewish themes appeared until the 1940s, after World War II and the Holocaust had sensitized Americans to the Jews in their midst. *Gentleman's Agreement* and *Crossfire*, both released in 1947, dealt with anti-Semitism.

On the Radio

While Jews were largely absent from the silver screen in the years preceding World War II, they appeared front and center in another entertainment medium—radio.

Jewish entertainers had been headliners in vaudeville, having gained experience on the stage earlier, in the Yiddish theater. Vaudeville was a tough business; only those who were quick on their feet, clever and tenacious

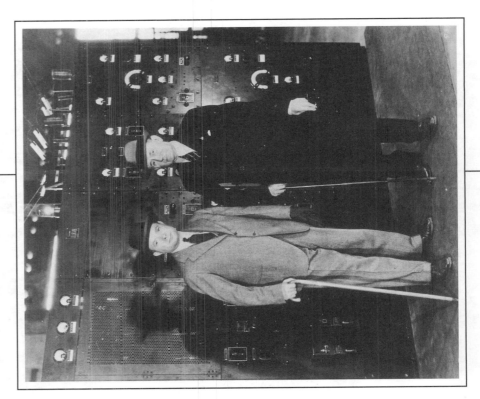

David Sarnoff, father of commercial broadcasting, with the legendary inventor Guglielmo Marconi at the RCA Communications Center on Long Island, New York, in 1933. In 1906 at the age of 15, Sarnoff went to work for the American Marconi Company as a telegrapher. His vision of radio as a mass communications service led to his creation of the National Broadcasting Company, which he headed for decades. *(National Portrait Gallery, Smithsonian Institution)*

Jack Benny (right), one of The United States' most beloved entertainers, performs for a group of admiring sailors. Like other entertainers, Benny spent much time during World War II traveling to entertain American troops. (Special Collections Department, University Research Library, UCLA)

succeeded. Vaudeville theater came to an end in the late 1920s, when it was replaced by broadcast media. The most successful vaudeville entertainers moved first to radio in the 30s and 40s and then to television in the 1950s while some became film stars.

Al Jolson easily transferred his popularity in *The Jazz Singer* to radio. Joining him were other Jewish performers such as Jack Benny, Ed Wynn, George Burns and Eddie Cantor. Jewish identity in their programs was usually limited to a Yiddish character. Eddie Cantor had The Mad Russian, and Jack Benny had Mr. Kitzel and Schlepperman. But for the most part, the comedians downplayed their Jewish connections.

Live radio provided some interesting, unrehearsed moments. For example, during one Jack Benny program, bandleader Phil Harris, also Jewish, bid farewell to Benny by saying "So long, Yankel"—the Yiddish version of Jack's Hebrew name. The Jewish audience felt comfortable with these characters and smiled at the success of fellow Jews. Rob Reiner, an actor and director commented, "Even if you're not Jewish, you can relate to this way of seeing the world."[5]

While their radio and television shows were wildly popular and brought a Jewish presence into every corner of America, the programs rarely displayed outward Jewish content. *The Goldbergs* was different. Beginning in 1930, it became one of the longest-running programs on radio, eventually moving to television. *Life* magazine wrote, "For millions of Americans, listening to *The Goldbergs*, a warm-hearted radio serial about a Jewish family, has been a happy ritual akin to slipping on a pair of comfortable old shoes that never seem to wear out."

Jack Benny (right) speaking with Walter Winchell. Born on the Lower East Side of New York, Winchell rose from singing for pennies on street corners to become one of The United States' best-known broadcasters. He also wrote a popular newspaper column. *(Special Collections Department, University Research Library, UCLA)*

The program was the continuing story of Jewish immigrants and their American-born children, Rosalie and Sammy, created by Gertrude Berg, who played the character Molly Goldberg. It was America's first soap opera, heard five times a week, for fifteen minutes a day.

While the adult characters spoke with accents and Mrs. Goldberg regularly fractured English sentence structure, it was a story to which all Americans could relate. "Yoo-hoo, Mrs. Bloom," Molly shouted to her unseen neighbor, and the night's episode began. For the first few years of the program Gertrude Berg played Molly with a heavy Yiddish style. "Oy, dere's mine bell vot's ringing," or "Vat's de matter so late, Sammy?" Later the accent was dropped, but the inverted sentence structure remained. As the years passed, the characters became increasingly Americanized, ultimately moving out of the Bronx to the suburbs.

After *The Goldbergs* was taken off the air, portrayal of Jews in radio and television sitcoms was limited, but beginning in the 1970s, Jewish characters seemed to be everywhere on television. There were plots with Jewish themes and a number of recognizably Jewish characters.

Their lives, however, did not reflect the reality of Jewish life in the United States. Jewish characters were never married to other Jews. Religious practices were barely mentioned. There were few scenes of Passover seders or traditional Sabbath observance. Many of the writers of

Rediscovering Yiddish

In 1980, a twenty-four-year-old graduate student, Aaron Lansky, realized that Yiddish books were being discarded by the thousands by American Jews who did not understand Yiddish, and so he organized a nationwide network to save the world's remaining Yiddish books from extinction.

The result is the National Yiddish Book Center, on the campus of Hampshire College in Amherst, Massachusetts. Since 1980, the center has collected 1.5 million volumes. It houses many of these titles and distributes others to university and research libraries around the world. The center is also the home of a theater and welcomes visitors to its many programs and activities.

the popular television shows were Jewish, and perhaps, like the film studio moguls of the 30s and 40s, they felt embarrassed by their Judaism or overly cautious about portraying Jewish life.

The Founders

In the early days of Hollywood, a small group of Jews founded America's leading film studios:

Carl Laemmle	Universal Pictures
William Fox	Twentieth Century Fox
Samuel Goldwyn and Louis B. Mayer	Metro-Goldwyn-Mayer (MGM)
The Warner Brothers	Warner Brothers
Harry Cohn	Columbia Pictures

Writing the American Story

Beginning early in the twentieth century, the course of American literature was changed by a succession of Jewish writers, most of whom were children of recent immigrants. The writings of Ludwig Lewisohn, Mary Antin and Abraham Cahan focused on their experiences in bridging the legacy of the European Jewish world with the reality of American life. Their books provided readers with insight into the struggles of Jewish immigrants to become "real Americans."

Mary Antin arrived in the United States in the 1890s at the age of thirteen. Her transformation from Yiddish-speaking immigrant from Polotsk, Poland, to respected American novelist began with the 1912 publication of her

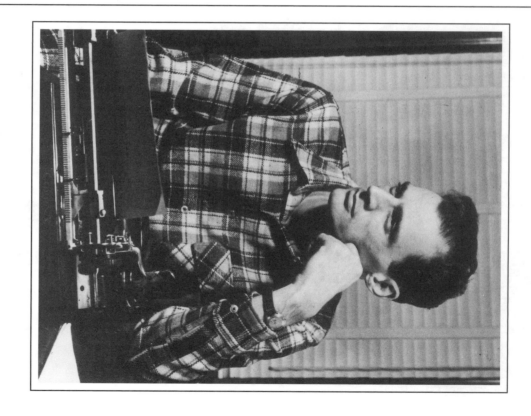

autobiography, *The Promised Land.* A reviewer wrote of one of her books: "Then and there Mary Antin became a good American, and we can take as many of their brethren who follow, for despite their poverty, uncouthness, and their shabbiness, they soon become better Americans than the natives themselves because they appreciate better what American means."[6]

Like other successful Jewish writers of the period, Antin credited the American public schools and libraries for her success. In *The Promised Land* she wrote:

That I, who was brought up to my teens almost without a book, should be set down in the midst of all the books that ever were written was a miracle as great as any on record. That an outcast should become a privileged citizen, that a beggar should dwell in a palace—this was a romance more thrilling than any poet ever sung.

Abraham Cahan was the legendary editor of the Yiddish-language newspaper, the *Forward*. Through its pages, he helped Americanize an entire generation of Jews. Cahan was also the author of the classic book *The Rise of David Levinsky*, published in 1917, which became the model for books written by other Jewish authors. The book traced the life of David Levinsky from poor immigrant to successful businessman, from the

Author Philip Roth. Roth was born in Newark, New Jersey, in 1933. His writing often reflects his Jewish roots. Among his best-known works are *Goodbye Columbus* and *Portnoy's Complaint*. He was the winner of the National Book Award in 1960 for *Goodbye, Columbus* and again in 1995 for *Sabbath's Theater*. In 1998, he was awarded the Pulitzer Prize for *American Pastoral*. (Library of Congress)

confines of the ghetto to his assimilation into main-stream society. It humanized the immigrant experience. Cahan, like Mary Antin, became among the first critical-ly acclaimed American Jewish writers to be accepted by a broad readership.

Both Antin and Cahan paved the way for other writ-ers who, as the century unfolded, expanded beyond the immigrant story. Although most of these later books do not outwardly deal with Jewish questions, they contain elements of their Jewish backgrounds. Many of their themes revolve around antiheroes and their discontent with the clichés of American life. Their books became popular classics and moved the authors into the literary mainstream. Works by Bernard Malamud, Edna Ferber, Lillian Hellman, Philip Roth and Saul Bellow are now firmly established as icons of American literature.

Indeed, many of their books became even more widely known when they were made into plays and movies. Malamud's *The Natural* and Ferber's *Showboat* and *Giant* were enjoyed by millions. Roth's *Goodbye, Columbus* raised questions about the direction American Jews were taking in their quest for acceptance. It appeared in 1959 at time when the American Jewish community was undergoing a population shift from the city to the suburbs. Roth's satire on the consumer orien-tation of upwardly mobile Jews mirrored real life for many Jews and non-Jews alike.

Books by these classic writers have been acclaimed worldwide. Ferber was awarded the Pulitzer Prize in liter-ature for *So Big*. Malamud received the National Book Award and the Pulitzer Prize for *The Fixer*, his fictional-ized story of Mendel Beilis, the Russian Jew falsely accused and later found innocent of ritual murder. Saul Bellow, who was born in Canada and then attended col-lege in the United States and stayed to write and teach, was awarded the Nobel Prize for literature in 1976.

Such well-known writers as Judy Blume, Paula

Theater poster for Arthur Miller's *Death of a Salesman*, his best-known play. The tragic story of salesman Willie Loman brought the playwright international fame. *(Library of Congress)*

95

Playwright Neil Simon, 1966. Simon was one of the most popular playwrights of the twentieth century. In 1970, three of his plays were performed simultaneously on Broadway. Several of his plays chronicled his own life: *Brighton Beach Memoirs* told of his childhood in Brooklyn, New York, where he was born in 1927; *Biloxi Blues* related his experiences as a soldier; and *Broadway Bound* dramatized his early success in the theater. *(Library of Congress)*

Danziger, E. L. Konigsberg, Robert Lipsyte and Mary Rodgers shaped young adult literature in the latter part of the twentieth century. They "helped to establish the flip, irreverent and dynamic tone that characterizes much of the contemporary realistic literature for young readers."[7] While their stories do not always contain outwardly specific Jewish components, they reflect the Jewish upbringing of the writers.

Their childhoods were not always religious. Author Milton Meltzer was typical: He described his parents as nonobservant; they rarely attended synagogue and didn't talk about being Jewish. "Nevertheless, their behavior . . . and their attitudes made an imprint that exposed the social history they brought with them."[8]

Laughter and Song Through Jewish Eyes

The world of popular comedy is filled with Jewish men and women whose works are familiar to all Americans. The movies of Woody Allen and the satire of Alan King, Jackie Mason and Elaine May set the stage for wildly successful television shows such as *Seinfeld* and *Mad About You*, in which Jews are portrayed

Was Superman Jewish?

Even the world of comic books owes much of its success to Jewish creativity. Two young Jewish men, Jerry Siegel and Joe Shuster, created *Superman* in the 1930s, just as the Nazis were coming to power in Germany. "It was no coincidence that Superman was created by Jews in a time of rabid anti-Semitism. Jews also created *Batman*, *Captain America*, and nearly every superhero that followed."[9] Many readers saw Superman's being rocketed from an exploding planet as an allegory of the Jews saving their lives by traveling to America, as their world in Europe was in peril.

Dr. Ivy Garlitz, a noted American-born British poet and expert on Jews and comics, wrote:

"Immigration comprises one of the most important elements in the Superman legend. In countless drawings, Superman stands proudly before the American flag, bearing the bald eagle on his arm. And yet, while holding him up as a model American, Superman stories reminded the reader that his powers came from his being an alien. Like other Americans, he is from 'the old country': in his case, Krypton. The portrayal of Superman's immigration in his stories provided readers with a mythologized view of their families' origins in other countries and their emigration to the United States."

98

Singer Barbra Streisand in concert, 1965. Streisand was born in Brooklyn, New York, in 1942. From the moment she entered show business, she was recognized as a superstar. She starred in Broadway plays, became a popular singer, actress, composer and film director. She has received numerous awards, including Emmys for her television work, Academy Awards for her films and Grammy Awards for her recordings. *(Library of Congress)*

unself-consciously. Many of the writers of these programs are Jewish but little of authentically Jewish religious and cultural life ever gets written into the scripts. The programs, perhaps reflecting the writers' own assimilation, emphasize the total absorption of American Jews into American life.

In one 1990s television series, *Love and War*, the Jewish character talks about his non-Jewish girlfriend. "Talk about peer pressure—I'm going to introduce Wally to the miracle of Hanukkah. And I want her to like it as much as she likes Christmas. That's a lie—I want her to like it more than Christmas. That way she'll convert—and then if we eventually get married, our children, Moses and Esther, won't be confused."

The American cultural scene has come a long way since *The Jazz Singer* of 1927. Jewish writers, artists, composers and entertainers continue to shape American arts. Steven Spielberg has become an icon of American filmmaking. His *Indiana Jones* series is legendary, and *Schindler's List* is arguably one of the more compelling Holocaust movies made. Other films, such as *Crossing Delancy*—a story of love—and *Once Upon a Time in America*—a vivid gangster tale—portray different facets of American Jewish life.

Many of the songs that fostered the rock-and-roll revolution were written by Jews and performed by black as well as white singers, including Elvis Presley, the Coasters and the Drifters. Only in America could songs such as "Spanish Harlem," "Yackety Yak," and "A Natural Woman" be written by Jewish composers and made famous by African-American singers. In the 1950s and 1960s, Jewish songwriters such as Neil Sedaka, Burt Bacharach and Carole King created over three hundred hit songs, adding to a new generation of Jewish contributions to American popular music.

Playing Ball? And You're Jewish?

Hank Greenberg's parents did not easily accept their son's choice of a career—that of a baseball player. Greenberg told a reporter in 1935 that "Jewish women on my block . . . would point me out as good-for-nothing, a loafer and a bum who always wanted to play baseball rather than go to school . . . I was always Mrs. Greenberg's disgrace."

But opinions changed when Greenberg made the National League. When he refused to play baseball on Yom Kippur, a reporter wrote, "He feels and acknowledges his responsibility as a representative of the Jews in the field of a great national sport, and the Jewish people could have no finer representative." Twenty years later, Sandy Koufax, star pitcher of the Dodgers, followed suit by refusing to play in an important World Series Game on Yom Kippur.

In 2000, Shawn Green, right fielder for the Los Angeles Dodgers, did not play in an important game that was played on Yom Kippur. "It's something I feel is an

Wrestler Bill Goldberg. By the end of the twentieth century, Jews could be found in careers well beyond stereotypical doctors, lawyers and professors. Bill Goldberg, a former football star at the University of Georgia, became one of the country's most popular professional wrestlers. (Associated Press)

Sports Hall of Fame

The International Jewish Sports Hall of Fame is located at the Wingate Institute in Israel. Here is a sampling of American Jewish members

Mel Allen	Sportscaster
Arnold (Red) Auerbach	Basketball
Jackie Fields	Boxing
Benny Friedman	Football
Hirsch Jacobs	Horse Racing
Sandy Koufax	Baseball
Benny Leonard	Boxing
Sid Luckman	Football
Al Rosen	Baseball
Abe Saperstein	Basketball
Dick Savitt	Tennis
Adolph (Dolph) Schayes	Basketball
Mark Spitz	Swimming
Sylvia Wene	Bowling

important thing to do," he said, "partly as a representative of the Jewish community, and as far as my being a role model in sports for Jewish kids, to basically say that baseball, or anything, isn't bigger than your religion and your roots."

Also that year, Gabe Kapler of the Texas Rangers said, "When all you have to look up to are producers, doctors and lawyers, it kind of cuts you off. It becomes education, education, education, which, don't get me wrong, is very important. But that's why we only have six Jews who are major league ballplayers. There needs to be more diversity in role models

John Frank, Jewish professional football player for the San Francisco 49ers. No category of Jewish professionals provided more joy to Jewish youngsters than sports figures. Although they were not widely represented, there were Jewish basketball, football and baseball players in professional sports beginning in the 1920s. *(Rauh Archives, Historical Society of Western Pennsylvania)*

for Jewish kids, and what's wrong with having them be strong and charismatic?"[10]

There have been few Jewish stars in baseball over the years, but they set high standards for themselves. Al Rosen, an All-Star third baseman for the Cleveland Indians in the 1940s and 50s, wanted everyone to know "here comes one Jewish kid that every Jew in the world can be proud of."

By the end of the twentieth century, fans were cheering Jewish athletes in diverse sports. Olympic gymnast Kerri Strug amazed everyone with her agility, while professional wrestler Bill Goldberg became a national favorite. Rabbi Aaron Kula, president of the National Jewish Center for Learning and Leadership, put it this way: "Maybe there is such a wide multiplicity to being Jewish we simply haven't named all the ways."[11]

CHAPTER 6

From *Heder* to Harvard:
The Lesson of
Henrietta Szold

"The school educates students to live as knowledgeable and committed Jews; to be intellectually curious, analytic and independent thinkers; and to adhere to the pluralistic ideals of our American democratic heritage."

FROM THE MISSION STATEMENT OF SOLOMON SCHECHTER SCHOOL, ESSEX-UNION, NEW JERSEY

The first generation of Jewish immigrants from Eastern Europe came to America with big dreams. But once here, they discovered that any hopes they had for themselves would have to be deferred to their children. "And all this time in a dismal tenement on the East Side in a gloomy, sooty room that looks more like a den than a dwelling place . . . they have pinned all their hopes to a son, an only grown-up son and that only grown-up son is going to take years to raise his family out of misery . . ."[1] In an article in a Yiddish newspaper, boys and girls from poor families were given practical advice. "... It is very well to dream of the professions, but remember that one does not nourish one's stomach with dreams...."

In the Europe left behind by the Jewish immigrant, highest praise was given to the scholar of Torah and Talmud. Once in America, however, immigrants found they were free from the religious pressures that had restricted their lives. In America, Jewish children had the

Orthodox rabbi teaching children. In the early part of the twentieth century, Jewish education of children took place in *heders*, or one-room schools. Although successful in Eastern Europe, these schools could not compete with the modern public schools in The United States. *(Library of Congress)*

Education for All

opportunity to live richer and more successful lives than their parents. The route out of the ghetto began in the local public school.

In Eastern Europe, either by custom or by law, public education was not often available to Jewish children. In the United States education was not only free, it was compulsory. The public school system was the route to becoming a "good American."

Jewish parents felt adrift in their new homeland. They were unfamiliar with the English language and customs of everyday life, and they were untrained in the cultural expectations of their American neighbors. To become "Americanized," many turned to a new educational institution, the night school. After ten- and fourteen-hour workdays at difficult jobs in sweatshop facto-ries, large numbers of immigrants voluntarily trudged into school buildings, community centers and settle-ment houses and opened textbooks to learn American history and the intricacies of the English language.

We are indebted to Henrietta Szold, the daughter of a prominent Baltimore rabbi, for the idea of the night school. Szold, who would later be an editor at The Jewish Publication Society and then founded Hadassah, the women's charitable organization, was a teacher at a pri-vate school. When Eastern European immigrants began arriving in Baltimore in large numbers during the 1880s, they were unfamiliar with American ways and language, and they embarrassed some in the established Jewish community.

Henrietta Szold realized that the new immigrants had to quickly learn basic English and new living skills if they were to succeed in their new country. There were no schools for adults and even if there had been, few if any students could have afforded to take time from their work to attend them. With support from others in the com-munity, Szold established the Russian Night School for adults in 1889, the first of its kind in the nation. Thirty men and women arrived on the first night, and within weeks, the number of classes had greatly increased, out-growing its small space. Szold served tirelessly as teacher, principal and fundraiser. She told a friend, "I eat, drink and sleep Russians."[2]

The following year the school moved to a small house with additional teachers, but even that proved inadequate for the growing number of students. Although the major subject taught was English, Szold introduced classes in American history, arithmetic, book-keeping and sewing. In 1898, the city of Baltimore took over responsibility for the school. So successful had been Henrietta Szold's experiment in educating poor, hard-working immigrants that her "Russian school" became a

School Days

In her book *The Promised Land*, Mary Antin described her first days in the public schools of Chelsea, Massachusetts.

"There were about half a dozen of us beginners in English, in age from six to fifteen. Miss Nixon made a special class of us, and aided us so skillfully and earnestly in our endeavors to 'see-a-cat,' and 'hear-a-dog-bark. . . .'"

Book learning was not all the children were taught. Entering school several decades later, writer Milton Meltzer remembered the efforts of his first grade teacher:

"Since some of us were foreign born, and most of us were the children of immigrants, the school assumed that the benighted countries we sprang from didn't know much about personal cleanliness. Sitting in our seats, while pantomiming the routines, we sang,

This is the way we brush our teeth, brush our teeth, brush our teeth,
This is the way we brush our teeth so early in the morning.'

To make sure we practiced what was preached, Miss Riley would now and then inspect each pupil's head of hair, and if lice were visible, it meant fierce scrubbing with harsh soap."[3]

model for other cities with growing immigrant populations. Educating newcomers became the responsibility of the public school system.

The same schools that provided immigrants' children with opportunities to succeed in America gave their parents a chance to become participants in their adopted country's culture and life. "The public school has done its best for us foreigners, and for the country, when it has made us into good Americans," wrote writer Mary Antin.

For most of the twentieth century, the descendants of these immigrants continued to champion the American public school system for their children. When a debate on expenditures for the New York City public schools arose in 1922, the Yiddish newspaper *The Day* responded, "It is a disgrace that the richest city in the world should not be able to provide adequate school accommodation for its children. . . ."[4] For most Jews, the public school was part of the very foundation of American democracy.

For many young Jews, the road from the public school led directly to the university. Children of poor immigrants took full advantage of the free higher education available at such public institutions as the City College of New York. By the end of the twentieth century, their descendents, in large numbers, continued the quest for higher education at the country's leading universities. Education was the key to a successful life in America. And while their grandparents had faced discrimination in the professions of medicine and law, there were no such barriers for their grandchildren.

The American Transformation of Religious Education

I n Europe, a young Jewish child's religious education was a normal part of growing up. It usually revolved around the one-room school—the *heder*, where the *melammed*, the teacher, taught the basics of the prayer book and the Bible by rote and by threat. The *heder* was not successfully transplanted to America.

In America, the chaider *assumes a position entirely subordinate. Compelled by law to go to the American public school, the boy can attend* chaider *only before the public school opens in the morning or after it closes in the*

Students at a Yiddish-speaking school in Pittsburgh, Pennsylvania, 1929. Members of the Yiddish Culture Society wanted their children to know and love Yiddish. By the end of the twentieth century, few Jews in the United States spoke or understood Yiddish. The language of the immigrants fell into disuse. *(Rauh Archives, Historical Society of Western Pennsylvania)*

"YEHOASH" FOLK SHULLE, MARCH 1929

afternoon . . . . Contempt for the chaider's teaching comes the more easily because the boy rarely understands his Hebrew lessons to the full. His real language is English, the teacher's is commonly the Yiddish jargon, and the language to be learned is Hebrew.[5]

The *heder* gave way to synagogue—or community—sponsored schools. Classes were held after the public school day and on Sundays. Community "Hebrew schools" provided students with improved curricula taught by trained teachers. The standards were higher than in the typical *heder* schools, where teachers were sometimes not knowledgeable of the subject matter and did not fully understood what it meant to be an American Jewish child.

The Kehillah in New York led the way to making religious education compatible with the public-school experiences of Jewish children. Samson Benderly, appointed by the Kehillah to direct its Bureau of Jewish Education, said, "What we want in this country is not Jews who can successfully keep up their Jewishness in a few large ghettos, but men and women who have grown up in freedom and can assert themselves wherever they are."[6] Benderly warned that "to withdraw our children from public schools and establish schools of our own as the Catholics are doing would be fatal (to the Jewish experience)."

The focus of most American Jews was on the public school education of their children. Since the majority lived in communities with high Jewish populations, reminders of their religious and ethnic culture constantly surrounded them. Yiddish was spoken in the streets. Everyone was familiar—even the most nonobservant—with religious practices and customs.

For most students, formal Jewish education ended with Bar Mitzvah. While the schools did their best to cram Hebrew language, Bible and religious training into the few hours allotted, the education for most Jewish children was basic and limited.

A survey in 1927 found that of 750,000 Jewish children in the United States, only 250,000 of them received some sort of Jewish education. The researcher who conducted the survey found that Jewish children "are ignorant of the most rudimentary questions concerning Jewish lore . . . even the Christian child knows more about ancient Judaism. . . ."[7]

Bureaus of Jewish education in the large cities developed standardized curricula, and trained and certified teachers. The bureaus represented the "the first systematic attempt to bring order out of the chaos of Jewish education in America."[8] Modern teaching techniques were instituted and the faculties largely consisted of American-trained, English-speaking teachers. The study of the Hebrew language was at the center of the learning. The technique of *Ivrit b'Ivrit*—teaching Hebrew by using Hebrew—introduced spoken Hebrew to students. For centuries, Hebrew had been reserved for studying Torah and prayer. With the growth of modern Zionism, Hebrew was revitalized as a spoken, everyday language.

After World War II, much of the Jewish population shifted away from the big cities. Reform and Conservative temples in the suburbs built their own schools, independent of the large city bureaus. Even as Jewish education became increasingly fragmented, other realities of American suburban life pressed upon the religious schools. No longer could children walk to religious school; they had to be driven, and so family life was organized around the carpool. And the demands of soccer practice, music lessons and after-school activities shortened religious school hours.

By the 1960s, Jewish assimilation into American mainstream culture had begun to sever connections to the previously cohesive Jewish world. Rabbi Irving "Yitz" Greenberg put it well when he said, "Freedom means the end of guarantees." No longer was there any certainty that children would have the same emotional ties to Judaism as their parents.

Temples cut back their hours of instruction to accommodate the increasingly hectic lives of suburban Jewish families. The "Hebrew school" experience for most Jewish children was the necessary route to Bar and Bat Mitzvah and generally stopped at age thirteen.

Jewish Day School Enrollment by Grade Level

While not accounting for students in preschool and specialized programs, these numbers show that the percentage of students decrease with each succeeding grade with more younger children enrolled in Jewish day schools than older students.

Grade	
1st Grade	9.04
2nd Grade	8.84
3rd Grade	8.70
4th Grade	8.30
5th Grade	7.87
6th Grade	7.49
7th Grade	6.83
8th Grade	6.41
9th Grade	5.53
10th Grade	5.13
11th Grade	4.68
12th Grade	4.10

Orthodox students comprise 80 percent of all Jewish day school students in the United States.[9]

Supplementary Jewish schools did provide an important foundation for children, but it was too little and too shallow. With the pressure to do well in public school and get into college, few chose to make the time for further Jewish education beyond the age of thirteen. As the typical American Jewish family became more secular and further removed from Jewish neighborhoods and culture, the already limited influence of the religious school waned even further. By the 1980s, concerned American Jews began to look for a new model of religious education for their children.

For years, the Jewish day school was almost exclusively a phenomenon of Orthodox Jewry. Its roots were in the European yeshivah, where boys received intensive religious education. (Girls were generally not admitted to Orthodox yeshivot.) In this country the yeshivah model was enlarged to include secular studies, but even here the focus for many decades was on religion. Its appeal to parents was very limited and consequently the number of students attending these schools was limited. Only with the arrival of large numbers of Orthodox Jews from Europe, before and after the Holocaust, did the Orthodox day school movement dramatically grow.

For most of the twentieth century, Jewish support of the American public school system was overwhelming. It had given Jewish immigrant children the tools with which to rise out of the ghetto and into the professions. It had allowed Jews to achieve "the American dream" within just one generation. Yet that very success was achieved at a price. Jewish children were growing up disconnected from their religious roots. And so a growing number of non-Orthodox parents looked to the day school model of the Orthodox community and began to establish Reform and Conservative day schools in their communities.

In the 1940s, less than twenty thousand students attended Jewish day schools, nearly all run by Orthodox

Judaism Goes to College

With large numbers of Jewish students attending college, Jewish studies departments at leading American universities now offer advanced courses in Jewish subjects, providing yet another opportunity for young people to connect to their heritage. Among them are:

Boston University
Brandeis University
Columbia University
Dartmouth College
Drew University
Emory University
Harvard University
Ohio State University

Princeton University
Stanford University
University of California at Los Angeles
University of Chicago
University of Connecticut
University of Pennsylvania
Yale University
Yeshiva University

For decades, independent degree-granting institutions of Jewish studies have been serving the Jewish community by training religious school teachers, communal workers and lay leaders. Among them are:

Baltimore Hebrew University
Cleveland College of
Jewish Studies

Gratz College, Philadelphia
Hebrew College, Boston
Spertus Institute, Chicago

groups. Since 1960, the number of Jewish day schools in the United States has tripled—providing education to of 200,000 students. The largest growth took place in Reform- and Conservative-sponsored schools. In 1997, eleven new Jewish high schools opened across the country.

In spite of this phenomenal growth, day schools serve only one-fifth of Jewish school-age children. Tuition costs are one reason. Another is the faith most American Jews still have in the public school system. A 1999 survey in Philadelphia revealed that while 18 percent of Jewish students there attended day schools, another 59 percent received their Jewish education in a supplementary temple school. The study also showed that another 22 percent were not receiving any Jewish education.

On the horizon for day schools are "boarding schools," which Rabbi Alvin Mars, the founding headmaster of the American Hebrew Academy in North Carolina, expects to be "the ultimate day high school—an all-day, all-week, all-school-year school." Rabbi Daniel Lehmann, Headmaster of the New Jewish High School in Waltham, Massachusetts, said such boarding schools will "create a total living environment like at camps."

Today, Jewish communities through their Jewish federations are re-evaluating their support for the day schools to make this type of educational available and affordable to more families. A study by the Avi Chai Foundation concluded the day school was "the only type of Jewish education that stands up against the very rapidly growing rate of assimilation."

Alternatives to Formal Jewish Education

I n spite of the growth of day schools, the vast majority of Jewish children attend public or secular private schools. As a result, parents in the 1980s began looking for alternative ways of connecting their children to the Jewish world. Jewish community centers have broadened their services to include courses in Jewish living and Hebrew language. Summer camps run by Orthodox, Conservative and Reform groups have grown steadily and have become extremely successful in immersing children in a total Jewish living experience. Trips to Israel for teenagers, increasingly subsidized by Jewish federations and private foundations, have strengthened the ties of young people to Israel and the Jewish community.

Bringing Jewish Literacy to Adults

As the debate continues over the most appropriate Jewish education for children, Jewish educational leaders have begun to look at the needs of their parents. The immigrants who arrived in America at the beginning of the twentieth century were illiterate in English and American culture. And now, at the beginning of the twenty-first century, their college-educated descendents have become increasingly Jewishly illiterate. Today, the model established by Henrietta Szold's "Russian School" has been recreated for a variety of educational programs targeting Jewish adults.

Adult Jews, now comfortable as Americans, are searching for opportunities to improve their understanding of Judaism, and synagogues and educational institutions are responding. They offer courses in Hebrew language and in religious studies for adults whose Jewish education stopped years earlier. Nationwide Hebrew literacy campaigns have attracted thousands. One rabbi said, "We have smart people coming into synagogues who are like children again because they open a book and can't read it. If we can help turn the Hebrew page into words that have meaning, it should radically change their experience."[10]

Organized programs such as Me'ah, developed at Boston's Hebrew College, provide busy adults with courses on Jewish history and important Jewish books. An

Jewish Studies In College

With 90 percent of all Jewish young people at the end of the twentieth century attending college, education today is still a high priority for American Jews. What has changed is a revitalized interest in improving Jewish education for the descendants of immigrants for whom a secular education was so important. Leading American universities now offer introductory and advanced courses in Jewish subjects as part of their general curricula. Jewish studies departments can now be found at many universities, large and small, around the country, where Jewish students have another opportunity to connect to their heritage.

interesting development is the number of women who participate. In earlier decades, girls and women were not encouraged to study Jewish texts. Speaking about the Me'ah program, Hebrew College president David Gordis said, "Women have emerged much more visibly both in positions of Jewish leadership and in prominence and have been re-empowered Jewishly. . . ."

As interest in Jewish education expanded, community leaders began focusing attention on ways to improve the quality and availability of Jewish educational options for both children and adults. The Jewish community is hard at work creating new day schools, improving supplementary education, and adding more adult and family programs.

Years of Despair:
The Riegner Telegram

"Indifference, then, is not only a sin, it is a punishment. And this is one of the most important lessons of this outgoing century's wide-ranging experiments in good and evil."

ELIE WIESEL

O n December 13, 1942, millions of Americans tuned their radios to Edward R. Murrow's regular newscast from World War II London. What they heard that evening shocked them. Murrow began his program in an almost melancholy way. By the time he finished, the world had heard the first broadcast accounts of the Holocaust.

One of the nice things about talking from London on Sunday night is that one can sit down, review the events of the week, study the reports coming in from all over the world, and then talk about whatever seems interesting . . . One is almost stunned into silence by some of the information reaching London. Some of it is months old, but it's eyewitness stuff supported by a wealth of detail and vouched for by responsible governments. What is happening is this: Millions of human beings, most of them Jews, are being gathered up with ruthless efficiency and murdered . . . It is a picture of mass murder and moral depravity unequaled in the history of the world. It is a horror beyond what imagination can grasp . . . The Jews are being systematically exterminated throughout all Poland . . . There are no longer concentration camps—we must speak now only of extermination camps.[1]

Murrow's powerful words, later proven sadly accurate, did not influence official thinking at the time. Most Allied leaders thought the reports greatly exaggerated. After all, Europe was fighting a terrible war, with heavy casualties on both sides. No one wanted to believe that the Germans, heirs to the cultural legacy of Beethoven and Bach, were systematically destroying an entire people.

Murrow's report was not the first public indication that something terrible was happening to the Jews of Europe. At a news conference weeks earlier, on November 28, 1942, Rabbi Stephen S. Wise announced similar reports of the Nazi plan to murder the Jews of Europe. The next day, *The New York Times* reported on Wise's announcement in a short article buried on page ten.

Rabbi Wise's information came from Gerhardt Riegner, the Swiss representative of the World Jewish Congress. In August, Riegner received undisputed confirmation about the Nazi killings. He immediately sent a telegram to Rabbi Wise in New York through the State Department's private courier service, to which President Roosevelt had given Wise access. Officials at the State Department thought the information was unbelievable. The American Embassy in Switzerland had forwarded the telegram to Washington with the following caution: "The report has earmarks of war rumor inspired by fear. . . ."

Rabbi Stephen S. Wise. Rabbi Wise was the best-known Jewish leader in the United States for the first half of the twentieth century. He was an active Zionist and a founder of the American Jewish Congress and of the National Association for the Advancement of Colored People. He was born in Hungary in 1874. After graduating from Columbia University, he was ordained as a rabbi. Wise said his role as a rabbi was "to plead for righteousness wherever and whenever unrighteousness obtains among men of earth and things of earth." (Library of Congress)

Afraid of hysterical public reaction, the State Department withheld the telegram from Wise.

Riegner, anticipating State Department inaction, sent a duplicate message to the World Jewish Congress office in London, which notified Wise by telegram on August 28, 1942:

. . . Received alarming report that in Führer's headquarters plan discussed and under consideration all Jews in countries occupied or controlled Germany numbering 3? to 4 million should after deportation and concentration in east at one blow exterminated to

resolve once for all Jewish question in Europe. Stop. Action reported planned for autumn. Methods under discussion including prussic acid. Stop. . . .

Rabbi Wise, upset that the original message had not been forwarded to him, confronted Sumner Welles, the undersecretary of state, who apologized and finally produced the telegram. Welles asked Wise not to publicize the contents of the telegram until the charges could be confirmed by independent sources.

By November, American diplomats had received further information about the mass extermination of Jews throughout Europe. Welles summoned Rabbi Wise to his office and handed him a pile of letters:

I regret to tell you, Dr. Wise, that these confirm and justify your deepest fears . . . For reasons you will understand, I cannot give these to the press, but there is no reason why you should not. It might even help if you did.[2]

Reporting the Unimaginable

Edward R. Murrow, America's best-known war reporter, was one of the first Americans to reach a liberated concentration camp. On April 12, 1945, he entered Buchenwald. Three days later he told listeners ". . . Murder had been done at Buchenwald," as he reported the graphic details of what he had seen. "I pray you," he concluded, "to believe what I have said about Buchenwald. I have reported what I saw and heard, but only part of it. For most of it I have no words . . . If I've offended you by this rather mild account of Buchenwald, I'm not in the least sorry."

Photos and films of the pitiful survivors and the stacks of still-unburied bodies flashed across newspapers and movie screens. Americans who had been focusing on bringing the war to an end could only then begin to understand the enormity of the crime.

The next day, Rabbi Wise held his news conference.

The Riegner telegram and the information that followed provided all the proof that was needed to substantiate the long-rumored German plan to kill all the Jews of Europe. Yet, news reports downplayed the enormity of the charges. It was wartime after all and millions of soldiers and civilians were dying. Most Americans could not comprehend the scale of Jewish murder.

Even when presented with firsthand witnesses, Americans could not bring themselves to grasp the enormity of what they heard. In September 1942, Jan Karski, a Polish diplomat—eyewitness to horrible acts committed against Jews—met with Supreme Court Justice Felix Frankfurter.

"Mr. Karski," Frankfurter asked, "do you know that I am a Jew? There are so many conflicting reports about what is happening to the Jews in your country. Please tell me exactly what you have seen." For the next thirty minutes Karski told Frankfurter gruesome details of what he had seen. When the diplomat finished, Frankfurter got up from his chair, paced silently for a few moments and then turned to his guests. "Mr. Karski, a man like me talking to a man like you must be totally frank. So I must say: I am unable to believe you."

The Polish ambassador, who had accompanied Karski, jumped up. "How can you call him a liar to his face! The authority of my government is behind him." Frankfurter answered softly, "Mr. Ambassador, I did not say this young man is lying. I said I am *unable* to believe him. There is a difference."[3]

Reaction to the Rise of Nazism

Even before coming to power in 1933, the Nazis made no secret about their hatred for Jews. Discrimination and violence against Jews escalated in Germany throughout the 1930s, and their rights were increasingly curtailed. In the United States, Jewish groups banded together after the German elections of 1933, which placed the Nazi party in power. The threat to German Jews brought the traditional Jewish defense agencies such as the American Jewish Congress, American Jewish Committee, the Jewish War Veterans and B'nai B'rith together. Mirroring the views of the American Jewish community, the groups could not come to a consensus on the appropriate actions to take.

B'nai B'rith and the American Jewish Committee feared that organized boycotts against German products might backfire "and kill Jews in Germany."⁴ The American Jewish Congress, led by Rabbi Stephen S. Wise, lobbied for a more activist course of public marches and mass meetings. On March 27, 1933, over 25,000 people filled Madison Square Garden in New York City. Thousands more jammed the surrounding streets as speaker after speaker rose to condemn the anti-Jewish actions in Germany.

Leaders of the Jewish community in Germany, fearing retribution, had urged the Americans not to protest. Yet in New York and in eighty other American cities Jews and non-Jews rallied. In New York, Bernard Deutsch, president of the American Jewish Congress, spoke for all who gathered to protest Germany: "We are overwhelmed with grief as we behold a situation, which if permitted to continue, would result in the descent of a great nation from a high state of enlightenment to a position of barbaric medievalism."[5]

While the American Jewish organizations disagreed on appropriate public response to the Nazis, they agreed on the need for diplomatic efforts. Representatives of the groups met frequently with officials at the State Department to urge an American response, but these private appeals produced little in the way of results.

Responses from members of Congress were more forthcoming. After a series of particularly bloody riots against Jews in 1935, Congressman Emmanuel Celler spoke out: "When are these brutalities to end? When will Germany cease her cowardly and diabolical attacks against a defenseless race? Surely the civilized nations cannot remain complacent while the Jews in Berlin live in constant terror of the Nazi raids."[6] Although reports of Nazi excesses against Jews appeared periodically in American newspapers, there was little editorial response until late in 1938. On November 9 and 10 of that year, violence against Jews broke out all over Germany in what came to be known as Kristallnacht or the Night of Broken Glass. The next day, American newspapers widely reported beatings of Jews, burnings of synagogues and imprisonment of innocent people. The lives of all German Jews were in peril.

The Voyage of the St. Louis

There were few escape routes. Strict immigration laws severely limited the number of Jews to the United States. Just months after Kristallnacht, the German ship, SS *St. Louis*, left Hamburg for Cuba with

The *Quanza's* Success Story

O n August 9, 1940, the Portuguese ship *Quanza* left Lisbon, bound for New York with over three hundred Jewish refugees aboard. Two-thirds of the passengers disembarked safely in New York and the ship continued on to Veracruz, Mexico, where the remaining passengers, holding valid Mexican visas, planned to go ashore. Like Cuba, Mexico refused to honor the visas and the passengers were not allowed to leave the ship.

Rabbi Wise turned to the State Department, which assured him it would monitor the situation. Wise then

930 Jewish passengers. When the ship reached Havana, the Cuban government refused to recognize the passengers' travel visas and refused them entry. Nazi propaganda used the incident to highlight world apathy toward the Jews of Europe. While the *St. Louis* slowly cruised along the coast of Florida, Jewish organizations tried unsuccessfully to obtain permission for the refugees to land in the United States. On June 6, the ship began a return voyage to Europe. Passengers received temporary refuge in European countries but many became victims of the Nazi Final Solution as German troops overwhelmed Europe.

The story of the SS *St. Louis* and its ill-fated passengers is well known. After the war, it was the basis of a successful play and film, *Voyage of the Damned*. In contrast to the fame of the *St. Louis*, the voyage of another ship less than a year later is hardly remembered. Yet, the passengers on this second ship realized the dream that passengers on the *St. Louis* never attained.

sent a letter to his friend and fellow Jew, Josephus Daniels, the United States Ambassador to Mexico, enlisting his help to aid the refugees. A few of the refugees were permitted to enter Mexico, but the ship was forced to turn back to Europe with the remaining refugees on board.

News reached the United States that the *Quanza* would be docking in Norfolk, Virginia, to take on a load of coal before crossing the Atlantic. Acting on behalf of a family aboard the ship, a Jewish Norfolk attorney, Jacob L. Morewitz, filed a libel suit in U.S. District Court against the ship's owners. Morewitz contended that the shipowner failed to comply with legal contracts to deliver the passengers safely to Veracruz. It was a gamble, but a federal judge ordered the *Quanza* impounded, thereby delaying the ship's departure. This gave supporters in the United States four days to marshal their forces on behalf of the refugees. During that time, the plight of the passengers was front-page news all over the country.

The most important supporter of the rights of the refugees was Eleanor Roosevelt. Concerned about the passengers, she arranged for influential American Jews such as Rabbi Wise and Congressman Sol Bloom to meet with State Department officials. When it was clear that the Secretary of State was not willing to back away from America's strict immigration rules, the First Lady turned to her husband.

Franklin Roosevelt was in the midst of a reelection campaign and did not want to provoke the anger of the large and vocal group of isolationists in and out of Congress who were strong opponents to any American involvement in another European war. Ultimately, despite strong objections from the State Department, Roosevelt's appointee to the President's Advisory Committee on Political Refugees, Patrick Murphy Malin, decisively ordered all the passengers released.

There is no doubt that the legal victory of Attorney

Morewitz saved the lives of the refugees. The judge in the case later wrote, "If the libels had not been filed against the *Quanza*, that vessel would very probably have left this jurisdiction . . . where the vessel would have proceeded thereafter, and what the libellants' fate would have been, no one can say. . . ." The joy was short-lived. The *Quanza* refugees landed safely in the United States but others could not. Immediately after Malin's decision, the State Department further tightened already strict immigration policies by eliminating the few loopholes available for saving European Jews.

Between Fear and Freedom

A number of German-Jewish professors, writers and scientists were able to reach the United States in the 1930s, thanks to efforts of private organizations in the United States. Edward R. Murrow, who worked for one of these organizations before becoming a news broadcaster, said, "The best education I ever received came from German professors who were flung out of German universities by Hitler."

These refugees were the lucky ones. Even as news of Nazi atrocities reached the United States, the State Department continued its strict immigration procedures, even going so far as to obstruct legal visa applications. In a June 26, 1940, memo to State Department officials, Breckinridge Long, the assistant secretary of state, advised American consuls "to put every obstacle in the way and to require additional evidence and to resort to various administrative devices which would postpone and postpone and postpone the granting of the visas."

The proud Zelkowitz family of Pittsburgh, during World War II. Jewish Americans have served in the United States' armed forces in every war since the Revolutionary War.
(Rauh Archives, Historical Society of Western Pennsylvania)

When Germany invaded Poland on September 1, 1939, Jews there became targets of roving killing squads of soldiers. Poland had one of the largest concentrations of Jews in Europe and the Nazis were soon overwhelmed by their mission to kill them all. As the Germans marched into other European countries the conqueror's "Jewish problem" increased.

On January 20, 1942, a meeting of Nazi officials met at a villa on the shore of Berlin's beautiful Wannsee. Without using the words "murder, extermination or death," they drafted the official German plan for the "Final Solution of the Jewish problem in Europe." At the time the world knew nothing of these plans. Only gradually did

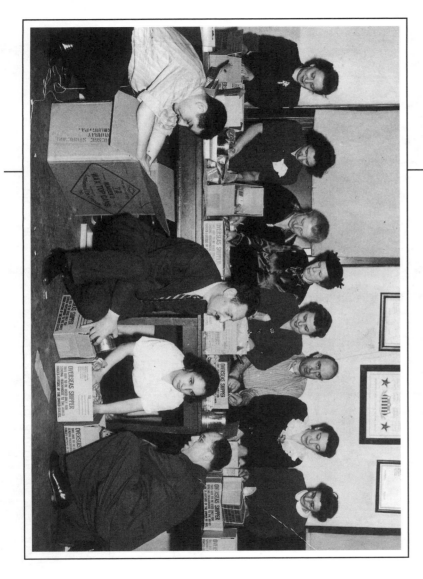

Packing supplies for American servicemen during World War II. Jews, like other Americans, mobilized during World War II to support American soldiers fighting overseas. (Rauh Archives, Historical Society of Western Pennsylvania)

governmental and Jewish groups begin to piece together what was really happening to the Jews of Europe.

The organized Jewish community in the United States worked diligently to save European Jews, but their ability was hampered by certain realities. First, American Jews at the time did not have an important political voice. They feared being thought of as "too pushy." Prior to Pearl Harbor, American sentiment was set against intervention in another "European war," and Jews did not want to be cast as warmongers.

Second, after the United States entered the war, the entire country focused on the main business of winning the war. Jews wanted to be viewed as loyal Americans who supported the national war effort. They did not want to appear overly critical about the lack of world action on behalf of Europe's Jews while millions of young Americans, Jewish and non-Jewish, were heading overseas to fight. Like most Americans at the time, Jews believed that the only way to close down the extermination camps was to win the war and put an end to the Nazis.

Rabbi Wise and others maintained frequent contact with the White House. In 1942, Wise led a committee to speak with President Roosevelt about the atrocities in Poland. "Mr. President," Rabbi Wise said, "we appeal to you, as head of our government, to do all in your power to bring this to the attention of the world and to do all in your power to make an effort to stop it." Roosevelt replied that the government was aware of the killings and then added, "We are dealing with an insane man— Hitler—and the group that surrounds him represents an example of a national psychopathic case . . . It is not in the best interest of the Allied cause to make it appear that the entire German people are murderers." Roosevelt then told the group:

It is not our purpose to fight for greater rights for anyone at the expense of another group. We are for the freedom for all and equal rights for all. We consider the attack on the Jews in Germany, in Poland, as an attack upon our ideas of freedom and justice, and that is why we oppose it so vehemently.

As the group prepared to leave the President's office, Roosevelt said, "We shall do all in our power to be of service to your people in this tragic moment." Unfortunately, those words had no impact on the millions of Jews facing certain death in Europe.

Speaking Up

In 1943, American Jewish organizations urged the Allies, the group of countries fighting the Nazis, to undertake a "program of rescue" for the Jews of Europe. The Joint Emergency Committee for European Jewish Affairs, headed by Rabbi Wise and comprised of the American Jewish Congress, American Jewish Committee, Synagogue Council of America, Jewish Labor Committee and rabbinical groups, proposed the creation of temporary sanctuaries for European Jews. "We would be less than frank," they wrote the undersecretary of state, "if we did not convey to you the anguish of the Jewish community of this country over the failure of the United Nations to act until now to rescue the Jews of Europe."

Some American Jews had little faith in the quiet diplomacy favored by Rabbi Wise. Zionists who looked to the creation of a modern State of Israel after the war adopted an active public relations campaign to pressure the United States government. Led by charismatic Peter Bergson (in reality a Palestinian Jew named Hillel Kook, nephew of Jerusalem's chief rabbi), a small group of Zionist activists staged successful plays, pageants and rallies to call American attention to the plight of European Jews. The intense lobbying by Bergson and his followers resulted in President Roosevelt establishing the War Refugee Board. The Board succeeded in saving the lives of 200,000 Jews through its rescue projects.

Although the United States knew what was happening in the killing camps of Auschwitz and Birkenau, the government did not act upon requests by Bergson and other Jewish groups to bomb the camps or the rail lines leading to them. In 1944, the assistant secretary of war wrote to the War Refugee Board that bombing these camps was not possible for a number of military and logistical reasons. He claimed that the prime mission of the air forces was to destroy Germany's industrial system: "The positive solution to this problem is the earliest possible victory over Germany, to which end we should exert our entire means."[8]

An interesting outcome of World War II was the quiet end to much of the rampant anti-Semitism that existed prior to American involvement in the hostilities. Many attribute this to the large numbers of Jewish soldiers who served in the American armed forces. Many Americans who had never even met a Jew were suddenly sharing space in the barracks or a foxhole with one. One wartime advertisement for war bonds stated, "Out where the bullets are flying, our boys—our American boys—do not care if a wounded buddy is Protestant, Catholic, or Jew, nor whether he is Negro or White."[9]

Remembering the Holocaust

In the 1998 Annual Survey of American Jewish Opinion, 76 percent of American Jews ranked Holocaust remembrance above celebration of Jewish holidays, Jewish study, synagogue services and Jewish organizational activity.

Going Public

With the war's end, Judaism was unofficially elevated to one of America's three major religions. Although Jews at the time were less than 4 percent of the American population, from that time onward, rabbis, Protestant ministers and Catholic priests received equal treatment at public affairs.

Jewish refugee children from Europe. Strict immigration laws prevented most Jews from escaping the horrors of the Holocaust. Only after the war were large numbers of them able to leave Europe to begin new lives in the United States. *(Library of Congress)*

Shipping Torahs to Europe immediately after World War II. Following the war, Jewish life in Europe was ruined. American Jews raised money and sent clothes, food, medicine and religious items to help Holocaust survivors rebuild their lives. *(Rauh Archives, Historical Society of Western Pennsylvania)*

After the war, due perhaps to some guilt Americans felt, American immigration laws were relaxed to allow some survivors of the Holocaust to enter the country. American Jews raised funds for the newcomers and helped them rebuild their lives. Yet, from 1945 until the mid-1960s, little public mention was made about Nazi-era events that led to the horrible deaths of six million Jewish men, women and children.

When a proposal was made in the late 1940s for a Holocaust memorial in New York, representatives of major Jewish organizations rejected the idea. They feared that other Americans would continue viewing Jews as victims. The memorial, they believed, would be "a perpetual memorial to the weakness and defenselessness of the Jewish people." The head of the American Jewish Committee wrote, "We must normalize the image of the

Jew . . . the Jew should be represented as like others, rather than unlike others. . . ."[10]

Some Jewish leaders decried the focus on the Holocaust. Steven Bayme of the American Jewish Committee said:

The vision of the Holocaust as centerpiece of Jewish identity suggests that our connection with our past is a connection of sadness, that being a Jew is a matter of commemorating terrible events. This is a very distorted focus on the Jewish historical experience and the meaning of being a Jew.[11]

Commemorating the Holocaust

Holocaust memorials can be found in communities across the United States. They exist to inform, teach and allow all people to remember that bigotry and hatred can lead to violence. Among the many memorials are the following:

C.A.N.D.L.E.S Holocaust Museum,
     Terre Haute, Indiana
Desert Holocaust Memorial, Palm Springs
El Paso Holocaust Museum and Study Center
The Holocaust Memorial, Miami
Holocaust Museum, Houston
Metropolitan Detroit Holocaust
     Memorial Center
Museum of Jewish Heritage, New York
New England Holocaust Memorial, Boston
San Francisco Holocaust Memorial
Virginia Holocaust Museum

In 1993, the U.S. Holocaust Memorial Museum opened in Washington, D.C. The presence of the museum on a plot of government-owned land near the historic Mall created controversy at first. Within the Jewish world, debate centered on whether building this museum took needed funds away from other needs of the Jewish community, such as education. Others debated the wisdom of putting an obviously Jewish museum in such a publicly historic setting, within sight of the Capitol and the Washington Monument. Each year since its opening, more than two million people have visited the museum.

Opinion concerning the Holocaust had shifted over the decades from a topic of near silence to a major component of American Jewish identity. The memory of the Holocaust years remains firmly rooted in the consciousness of American Jews. Holocaust memorials have sprung up in cities all over the United States, from Boston to Miami to Los Angeles. Together with deep concern for Israel and the plight of Jews in the Soviet Union, the Holocaust has become a focal point of fundraising, programming and political activism.

Still Fighting Anti-Semitism

With the passing decades, anti-Semitism in the United States has dropped dramatically. Nonetheless, the 1998 Annual Survey of American Jewish Opinion indicated that Jews believed "by a margin of 57 percent to 38 percent that anti-Semitism is a greater threat [to . . . the survival of American Jews] than mixed marriage."

The perception of anti-Semitism remains strong within the American Jewish community, although bla-

In 1996, the United States Postal Service issued a special Hanukkah stamp for the holiday season. *(Hanukkah stamp, U.S. Postal Service)*

tant hatred against Jews is limited to a small number of extremist groups. Organizations such as the Anti-Defamation League and the Southern Poverty Law Center carefully monitor the activities of these hate organizations. "We have to shine a light on these groups," said Mark Potok of the Southern Poverty Law Center, adding that parents must talk to their children about racism, anti-Semitism and Holocaust denial.[12]

Shooting in Los Angeles. Even though Jews are becoming more accepted in American life, pockets of anti-Semitism prevailed. On August 19, 1999, a racist sprayed the lobby of the North Valley Jewish Community Center in Los Angeles with gunfire. Five people were wounded, including three small children. *(Associated Press)*

American Jews and Israel:
The Six-Day War and New Relationships

"Terror and dread fell upon Jews everywhere. Will God permit our people to perish? Will there be Another Auschwitz, another Dachau, another Treblinka?"

RABBI ABRAHAM
JOSHUA HESCHEL

I n late May and early June 1967, war in the Middle East seemed inevitable. From Arab countries came shrill sounds of hate and threats of impending war against Israel. The young nation had survived two major wars and an ongoing series of guerilla attacks since its birth in 1948. A new war could prove disastrous for the Jewish state. By early June 1967, Israel was surrounded by a combined Arab force of two hundred fifty thousand trained soldiers, two thousand tanks and seven hundred military aircraft. Fears of a new Holocaust were in the minds of American Jews.

Threats escalated. Egyptian President Gamel Abdel Nasser announced to frenzied crowds, "The army and all the forces are now mobilized . . . We are ready for war!" Despite earlier assurances, Israel's major allies—the United States, England and France—were reluctant to offer more than moral support. Israel's defense minister Shimon Peres was realistic. "The United States would never come to the defense of Israel. We have to defend ourselves and we know it."[1]

Rabbi Abraham Joshua Heschel wrote, "Terror and dread fell upon Jews everywhere. Will God permit our people to perish? Will there be another Auschwitz, another Dachau, another Treblinka?" Indeed, Arab leaders threatened to annihilate the Jews of Israel. One Arab officer calmly explained that after an Arab victory, "those [Israelis] who survive will remain in Palestine. I estimate that none of them will survive." "Many Jews would never have believed," Arthur Hertzberg wrote in the August 1967 issue of *Commentary*, published by the American Jewish Committee, "that grave danger to Israel could dominate their thoughts and emotions to the exclusion of all else."

Across the United States, Jews held mass meetings and rallies in support of Israel. Jewish groups such as the American Jewish Committee, which had never been a strong supporter of a separate Jewish state, joined with

Fighting for Freedom

With Israel fighting for its very existence in the 1948 War of Independence, a number of American Jews who had fought in World War II went to Israel's aid. They brought with them the expertise they learned as members of the United States armed forces.

The best known of them was Colonel David "Mickey" Marcus, a West Point graduate who was commandant of the U.S. Army's Ranger School during the war.

In 1947 he was asked to train soldiers in the fledgling Israeli army for the expected war with the Arab armies. David Ben-Gurion, Israel's first prime minister, conferred on Marcus the rank of general, making the American soldier the first Jewish leader of a Jewish army in two thousand years. Unfortunately, Marcus was killed accidentally one night by an Israeli sentry. Marcus, who spoke no Hebrew, could not give the guard the correct Hebrew password. "Mickey" Marcus was buried with honors at West Point.

Legendary broadcaster Edward R. Murrow, interviewing David Ben-Gurion, Israel's first prime minister, for a CBS television program. Since the birth of CBS Photo in 1948, Americans have maintained a high interest in Israel and happenings in the Middle East. *(CBS Photo)*

other Jewish religious and communal organizations to raise money and exert pressure on the American government to support Israel.

American Jews who had never considered themselves Zionists were personally moved by Israel's dire situation. "It was a foregone conclusion," John Slawson, head of the American Jewish Committee, told his staff, "that the combined forces of Egypt, Jordan and Syria would penetrate and be able to destroy Israel. What could we do?"[2]

War began on June 5, 1967. Israel unleashed a series of coordinated surprise attacks against Egyptian air bases, virtually destroying Egypt's air force. By the fourth day of the war Israel had completely shattered Egypt's armed forces. Four hundred Egyptian tanks were destroyed and two hundred more captured. Ten thousand Egyptian soldiers were dead and another twelve thousand taken prisoner. With the destruction of the Egyptian army, Israel turned its attention to the armies of Jordan and Syria. In fierce fighting the Israelis gained control of much of the West Bank of the Jordan River. On

The Renewal of Jewish Pride

June 7, Israeli paratroopers entered the Old City of Jerusalem and reclaimed the Western Wall. Since 1948, the Jordanians had controlled that part of Jerusalem and had forbidden Jewish access to Judaism's holiest site.

In the north, Israel gained control of the Golan Heights from whose fortified villages Syria had been able to shell Israeli settlements at will. By June 10, Israeli armor was on the way to Damascus, Syria's capital. The world looked on in amazement as Israel emerged victorious—just six days after the war began. Arab leaders at first refused to believe that Israel had acted alone and accused the United States of fighting for Israel. Egypt's President Nasser complained, "The enemy was operating an air force three times its normal strength!"

F or two thousand years, since the destruction of the Second Temple in Jerusalem and exile from their land, Jews had been outsiders wherever they lived. The image of a poor, defenseless and unempowered people accompanied Jews from country to country. They were expelled from Spain and other countries, restricted to ghettos and victimized by violence and discrimination. The irrational hate of anti-Semitism reached its peak in the mid-twentieth century, in the Holocaust.

With the stunning 1967 Israeli victory, Jews around the world experienced a renewed connection to their religion and to Israel. Many felt they had witnessed a religious miracle. They internalized the Israeli victory as their own. American Jews told stories of non-Jewish friends saying to them, "You really showed them." Jewish self-pride swelled.

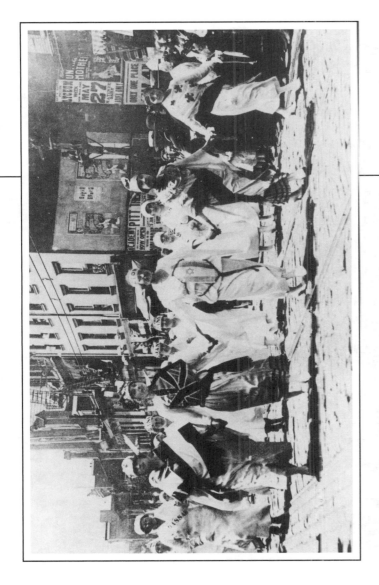

Declaration parade in Pittsburgh, Pennsylvania, 1917. Zionism was given a boost when the British issued the Balfour Declaration in 1917, which recognized the need to establish a Jewish state in Palestine. (Rauh Archives, Historical Society of Western Pennsylvania)

In spite of the joy and relief, Jews remembered the difficulties they faced in reestablishing the Jewish state just decades earlier. The birth of the State of Israel in the aftermath of the Holocaust did not dispel the image of Jews as powerless and defenseless. Even though it survived major wars in 1948 and 1956, Israel was still viewed as an underdog nation. But then, in six days in 1967, Israel suddenly found itself transformed into a Middle East superpower.

Before 1948, American Jewish support for the establishment of the State of Israel was not universal. Many ultra-Orthodox and Reform Jews opposed the Zionist agenda. The ultra-Orthodox believed that only God could reestablish a Jewish state. Reform Jews feared accusations of "dual loyalty" that would raise questions about their Americanism. The Reform movement's Union of American Hebrew Congregations, composed largely of Jews deeply assimilated into American life, had declared in an 1898 statement, "The Jews are not a nation but a religious community . . . America is our Zion."

142

President Harry Truman with his friend Eddie Jacobson. At a time of limited political access, Jews often depended on friendship to make their needs known. Jacobson played an important role in convincing Truman to support the fledgling State of Israel in 1948. *(Harry S. Truman Library)*

But this sentiment changed with the great influx of Eastern European Jews. The Zionist movement in the United States strengthened, and ironically, its major leaders were Reform Jews, including Rabbi Stephen S. Wise, Rabbi Abba Hillel Silver and Supreme Court Justice Louis Brandeis.

When World War II ended, the tragedy of the Holocaust led Jews to the inescapable conclusion that it was time for a Jewish state. American Jews mobilized their support. Membership in the Zionist Organization of America topped 500,000 by 1948, and financial contributions exceeded $200 million. This sum was four times as much as Americans gave to the Red Cross that year. American Jews lobbied members of Congress and the president, held mass demonstrations and raised funds. Between 1946 and 1962, more than $1 billion was raised through the United Jewish Appeal, the central fund-raising agency for Israel. Since the founding of Israel Bonds in 1951, more than $10 billion worth of bonds have been sold.

Once Israel was established in 1948, the majority of American Jews maintained their commitment to the survival of the fledgling country. Most did not go so far as to "make aliyah" (return to live in their ancient homeland), but in economic and political ways, their support was invaluable. Within a decade of Israel's founding, there were no less than eighteen major American Jewish organizations dedicated to Israel's support. In a short period of time, American Jews created a politically powerful network to advocate for Israel in Washington. It developed into an interlocking organizational system that brought the American Jewish community together.

This same network was instrumental in persuading the American government to support Israel. It was

Israeli Prime Minister David Ben-Gurion (center) and Ambassador Abba Eban (right) present President Truman with a Hanukkah menorah. Since its birth in 1948, Israeli leaders have tried to maintain close relations with the United States. Israelis and Jews everywhere were grateful for Truman's support in establishing the Jewish state. *(Harry S. Truman Library)*

143

Jewish support for Israel. Continuing tensions in the Middle East at the end of the twentieth century evoked memories of Israel's troubled past. Whenever Israel has been threatened, American Jews have rallied support. *(Associated Press)*

responsible for President Harry Truman's early recognition of Israel in 1948. And its lobbying led to the supply of desperately needed arms for Israel in the 1967 and 1973 wars by Presidents Lyndon Johnson and Richard Nixon.

From the beginning, Israel's problems seemed almost insurmountable. Massive immigration, poverty and lack of a working economy were only part of the problem. The young country was engaged in a continual struggle for survival in the midst of declared and undeclared wars by its Arab neighbors. Before 1967, Israel had fought two major wars—in 1948 and 1956—and faced relentless terrorist violence from across its borders. Although American Jews were supportive of Israel before the Six-Day War, few visited the Jewish state. Their energies focused largely on their own Jewish community. The

United Jewish Communities

Former Vice President Al Gore, speaking to the United Jewish Communities General Assembly in Georgia in 1999. Gore pledged to the almost 5,000 Jewish leaders from 189 Jewish Federations around the world that the United States would always stand by Israel "whenever she takes risks for peace." (Associated Press)

1950s and 1960s saw movement to the suburbs and the building of new synagogues and multipurpose Jewish community centers. Thoughts of the Holocaust and Israel took second place until the Six-Day War, when both issues overtook other concerns as the prime ways in which Jews identified themselves.

David Clayman, director of the Israel office of the American Jewish Congress, said, "Israel played a critical part in the American Jewish community preserving itself. Fundraising was the key. You worshiped at the altar of Israel by contributing. Jewish observance was raising money, not going to the synagogue."[4] Since 1967, as overt anti-Semitism declined and Jews were accepted into more areas of American life, Israel and the Holocaust became "substitute religions" that American Jews used to define themselves.

A Political Strategy for Peace

A merican Jewish support for Israel was at least partially responsible for involving American presidents in the quest for peace in the Middle East. The Yom Kippur War in 1973 began badly for Israel. To ensure United States support, Israel agreed not to fire the first shot as it had in the Six-Day War. Consequently, Israel suffered dramatic initial losses. The administration of President Richard Nixon was slow in responding to pleas for help from Israel. Secretary of State Henry Kissinger later explained, "I was determined to use the war to start a peace process." While he did not want to see Israel defeated, he also did not want the Arab states humiliated as they were in the 1967 war.

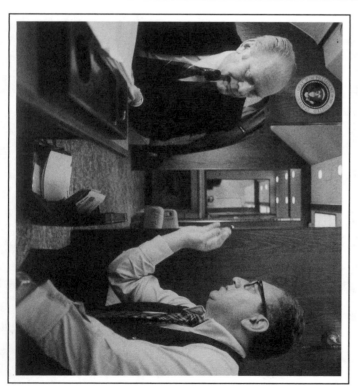

President Gerald Ford (left) with Secretary of State Henry Kissinger. Kissinger was the first Jewish U.S. Secretary of State. He was instrumental in breaking the diplomatic logjam in the Middle East that eventually led to peace treaties between Israel, Egypt, Jordan and the Palestinians. *(Gerald R. Ford Library)*

President Ford and Secretary of State Kissinger meet with leaders of the American Jewish community. By the 1960s, Jewish organizations had become confident enough to make their opinions on Jewish interests known to government officials. Leaders of the most important Jewish groups organized themselves to avoid duplication of lobbying efforts. (*Gerald R. Ford Library*)

The American Jewish community sprang into action with fundraising and lobbying efforts. In the first week of the war, they raised over $100 million. "It's a spontaneous uprising," one Jewish leader said. Ultimately, when the United States became convinced that Israel was really in trouble, President Nixon ordered a round-the-clock airlift of desperately needed replacement arms and ammunition. Israel survived another major threat to its existence, but the balance of power in the Middle East shifted again. Both sides realized there had to be a movement toward peace.

At 8 P.M. on November 19, 1977, an Egyptian airliner arrived at Israel's Ben-Gurion Airport. As television cameras broadcast the scene worldwide, Egyptian President Anwar Sadat stepped onto Israeli soil and was warmly greeted by Israeli Prime Minister Menachem Begin. The long-awaited peace process between Israel and her Arab neighbors was underway. In the years that followed, Israel signed peace treaties with Egypt, Jordan and the Palestine Liberation Organization. Israel was no longer isolated.

There were still major problems. Key among them was the fact that a Palestinian population was being ruled by Israel, on territory occupied since the Six-Day War. While negotiations about the creation of a Palestinian state continued, American Jews and many Israelis were discomforted and embarrassed by the public role of Israel as occupier. The long-drawn-out peace process brought out divisions between American Jews and Israelis. Eliahu Ben-Elissar, a former Israeli ambassador to the United States, said:

> There's a sharing of a sense of the same fate and destiny, a deep, deep feeling of belonging to the same people . . . the same moral values, knowing that in one's heart one cannot be without the other. At the same time [we're] having a lot of problems, a lot of problems which, may I say, are very Jewish.[5]

When suicide Palestinian bombers began a terror campaign against Israeli civilians in 2000, the peace process came to a crashing halt. This uprising resulted in military responses by Israel and even long-time activists for peace saw no hope of a meaningful resumption of negotiations. Yet the hope for peace continued.

The influx of highly trained Jews from the former Soviet Union in the 1980s and 1990s greatly benefited Israel's economy. One result has been less reliance on the financial support of the American

When the Going Gets Tough

A major source of revenue for Israel is tourism, especially by Jewish visitors. When Palestinian violence erupted in 2000, it not only ended the fragile peace process but dramatically affected Israeli tourism.

In February 2000, before the violence began, 37,484 Americans visited Israel. A year later, that figure dropped to 21,832, a 42 percent decline.[3]

Jewish community. Local Jewish federations began allocating a larger proportion of their funding away from Israel to needed social services and educational needs at home. With high intermarriage rates and low Jewish literacy, American Jews in the 1990s became concerned with "Jewish continuity" and the need to focus on religious education.

The Changing
Perspective on Israel

In the decades after the Six-Day War, there was a noticeable trend away from the traditional support of Israel by younger American Jews. Less than one-third of American Jews have even visited Israel.

Unlike previous generations who looked upon Israel as the young reincarnation of two thousand years of diaspora dreams, a pioneer society of Jews reinventing themselves, or even as a spiritual center of Judaism, these younger American Jews have lived with an Israel that is fifty years old, powerful militarily, and economically robust and increasingly intoxicated with American popular culture. This is an Israel that is far more independent and harder to romanticize or even to connect with as powerfully as their parents once did.[6]

American Jews today are in the process of reinventing themselves. They are less apt to identify with the tra-

The Pollard Affair

The Pollard affair in 1985 forced American Jews to consider their unique relationship with Israel. Jonathan Jay Pollard, an ardent supporter of Israel and a civilian intelligence analyst for the United States Navy, was arrested for espionage. He was accused of and readily admitted to providing thousands of classified documents to Israel. Most American Jews shared his idealistic concern for Israel's survival, but they were aghast that an American Jew would go so far as to commit espionage. Israeli Prime Minister Yitzhak Rabin called Pollard's action "a real disaster, a real wound in Israeli-U.S. relations." Pollard was sentenced to life imprisonment with no chance of parole. Since then, many American Jews have been lobbying the government to reduce Pollard's sentence, claiming that his punishment is excessive.

ditions of their parents' Eastern European Jewish heritage and the early events of the modern State of Israel. The near unanimous support among American Jews for the creation of Israel in 1948 and in the aftermath of the Six-Day War has subsided. Although most American Jews today continue to support Israel, they view the Jewish state less emotionally than before. Yet even when Israel faces renewed terrorist violence, most American Jews continue to support the continuation of a meaningful peace process. Although they acknowledge their Jewish heritage and have an emotional connection to the Jewish state, today's American Jews are looking for new ways to define their Jewishness and their connections to Israel.

Many American Jews and their organizations continue to provide traditional support to Israel. The strongest ties come from the Orthodox community, which sends students to Israel for yeshivah study, has a high rate of aliyah (moving to Israel) and has relations with Israel's religious establishment. The American Israel Public Affairs Committee remains one of the most successful lobbying groups in Washington.

Who Is a Jew?

Two presidents: Harry S. Truman and Chaim Weizmann, 1948. Since Truman's early and forceful recognition of Israel, every American president has supported the Jewish state. Truman in particular was credited with giving the fledgling country a boost by instantly recognizing Israel. (Harry S. Truman Library)

Despite these close ties, the "who is a Jew" question complicates relations. The Orthodox community in the United States numbers less than 10 percent of the Jewish population. In Israel, the percentage is only slightly higher, yet Orthodoxy there holds a monopoly on the religious life of all Israeli Jews, including birth, marriage and death. This is a result of a compromise with the religious community instituted by the British during their Mandate years in Palestine, prior to 1948. Its legacy continued in the new State of Israel to avoid political friction at a time when the fledgling state faced military and economic crisis.

When the Orthodox leadership in Israel, with its strong political connections within the government, attempts to delegitimize and block religious activity of Reform and Conservative rabbis in Israel, most Jews in the United States feel rejected and disappointed. Rabbi Ismar Schorsch, chancellor of the Conservative movement's Jewish Theological Seminary of America, explains it this way: "Jews in Israel and in the Diaspora can no longer avoid confronting the question of how a Jewish state dominated by the Orthodox can serve as the center of the Jewish world, where the Orthodox are only a small part of the population."[7]

New Connections to the Ancient Homeland

Since the Six-Day War, a number of new programs have been created to foster a closer relationship between younger American Jews and Israel. Jewish community centers in many American cities and Jewish summer camps throughout the country offer summer Israel experience programs and employ young Israelis on their staffs. Programs such as Birthright Israel, a collaboration of several philanthropists and the United Jewish Communities, provide free or low-cost trips to Israel for thousands of young American Jewish students each year. The hope, according to a Birthright organizer, is that "pride in Israel can translate into Jewish connection back home. That sense of pride will hopefully open doors into people's minds and inspire [participants] to take a Jewish class or a program at the JCC or Hillel. Life is full of these kinds of little decisions."[8]

Toward Religious Equality for Women and Gays: The Ordination of Sally Priesand

> *"Judaism is always changing. Reform means that Judaism is always in the process of becoming. It is never a state of being. It is always a relentless going on."*
>
> RABBI
> ALEXANDER
> SCHINDLER

Contrary to popular belief, the Bat Mitzvah celebration for girls is not a centuries-old Jewish tradition. Unlike the Bar Mitzvah ceremony for boys, the popularization of the Bat Mitzvah can be traced back to 1922. That year, at a regular Sabbath service, Rabbi Mordecai Kaplan, founder of Reconstructionist Judaism, called his daughter, Judith, before his congregation. There she recited the blessings before and after the reading of the Torah and read a section of the Torah in Hebrew and English. Within a few years, the Bat Mitzvah service had become an integral part of most Reform and Conservative congregations. And modern Orthodox congregations developed their own versions of the ceremony for girls that did not include a Torah reading.

Early Jewish Feminists

The traditional role of women in Judaism was limited to the home. They were exempted from many of the ritual commandments that were obligated to men, and they were not counted in a minyan, a minimum of ten men required to recite public prayer. In the synagogue, they did not wear prayer shawls and did not publicly participate in the prayer service or read from the Torah. In fact, women sat apart from the men in the synagogue, separated by a *mechitzah*, a room divider. It was not until the late nineteenth century that the *mechitzah* was removed from Reform synagogues and women were permitted to sit with men during services.

In traditional homes, it was the woman's job to maintain the home and raise the children. For most of the twentieth century, work outside the home for educated women was limited to the typically "female" occupations of teaching and social work. Although their roles were sometimes taken for granted, on Friday nights men for centuries rose from the Sabbath table to honor their wives by reciting from Proverbs the section that begins, "What a rare find is a capable wife! Her worth is far beyond that of rubies."

A few women escaped the traditional role. Henrietta Szold was one of them. A scholar and editor of Jewish studies, she was a respected speaker on religious themes and became the first woman admitted to the Jewish Theological Seminary—but with the agreement that she could never be ordained as a rabbi.

By the end of the twentieth century, the walls of traditional Jewish male superiority in Judaism had crumbled. In the more liberal Reform and Conservative movements, women served as rabbis and in elected and appointed positions in their own temples. Language changes made some prayer books gender neutral.

Cracks also began to appear in the modern Orthodox world in the 1980s, as women gathered in Torah study groups. Blu Greenberg, a respected Orthodox feminist, said, "Something that was unacceptable a generation ago, now is part of a girl's birthright." To those who argued that the women's groups were operating outside of *halakhah*, traditional Jewish law, Greenberg added, "Women's *tefilah* [prayer] is not minyan. It is *tefilah*."[1] Simply put, women are free to pray at any time and with anyone they wish.

Before other avenues opened for them, women participated in synagogue life through ladies' auxiliaries and sisterhoods. These groups not only provided social opportunities for their members but education and opportunities for social service as well. In 1918, Mathilde Schechter, wife of Solomon Schechter, head of the Jewish Theological Seminary, founded the Women's League for Conservative Judaism. "We wish to serve the cause of Judaism," she said, "by strengthening the bond of unity among Jewish women and by learning to appreciate everything in Jewish life . . . the self-education of Conservative Jewish women is only the first step toward the better education of our children." Women's groups in other branches of Judaism also developed opportunities for their members to fulfill their potentials as people and Jews. The National Council of Jewish Women, led for many years by Hannah G. Solomon, provided further opportunities for Jewish studies and political activism. More activity was to be found in such pro-Zionist organizations as the Pioneer Women (now known as Na'amat), Mizrachi, and the largest of all Zionist groups, Hadassah.

Jewish women who had been active in the abolitionist movement of the nineteenth century, working to bring an end to slavery, were also among the earliest feminist leaders in the United States. The names of Ernestine Rose, Lillian Wald and Emma Lazarus are well known.

Their greatest dream was realized in 1920 when women in the United States finally won the right to vote.

By the late 1960s and early 1970s women began to challenge their second-class status in American society. In spite of advances in the workplace, they were paid less than men were for the same jobs, and had little promise of advancement. Despite their good education they encountered institutional roadblocks that confined their talents to the home or to relatively low employment positions.

A growing feminist movement actively worked to gain equal rights for women in all aspects of life. Betty Friedan's book

The Feminine Mystique sparked the revolution in which Jewish women played prominent roles.

Bella Abzug was an early leader of the feminist movement. Like Henrietta Szold decades earlier, she became aware of the limitations on women within Judaism upon the death of her father. As a woman, she could not recite the *kaddish* prayer (the prayer for the dead) for him; traditional Jewish law prohibited it. "I went to the synagogue," she later recounted, "and I did it, though I wasn't supposed to. I learned that I could speak out and no one would stop me."[2]

Active in the anti-Vietnam war movement of the late 1960s, she successfully ran for Congress in 1970 under the slogan, "This Woman's Place Is In the House—The House of Representatives." As a member of Congress she introduced bills calling on the Soviet Union to allow the free emigration of its Jewish citizens, who were suffering from discrimination and anti-Semitism. After Sally

Supreme Court Justice Ruth Bader Ginsburg. In 1960, Ginsburg was recommended as a law clerk to Justice Felix Frankfurter, but he refused her. Frankfurter was not ready to appoint a woman to the position. (United States Supreme Court)

Priesand's ordination as the first woman rabbi in 1972, Abzug arranged for her to deliver the opening prayer at the House of Representatives. "She was the first Jewish woman to do so. Abzug said, " At that moment, I felt that two movements for social progress had merged and come of age. And I really felt at home in Washington."[3]

Women Rabbis

I n 1899, a Jewish reporter, Mary M. Cohen, wrote a short article, "Could Not Our Women Be Ministers?" in which she explored the then far-fetched idea of a Jewish woman becoming a rabbi. Women had been admitted as students at the Jewish Theological Seminary for decades. Many of them went on to successful careers as educators, social workers and communal workers. Even though several of them taught rabbinical students at the seminary, none of the women themselves were allowed to seek ordination as rabbis.

At the 1972 conference of the Conservative movement's Rabbinical Assembly, members of the women's study group Ezrat Nashim presented a "Call for Change" to the rabbis. They demanded a greater voice for women in religious services and inclusion in the count for a minyan. "We had received equal education in Conservative synagogues along with men," Paula Hyman, one of the members, said, "but at a certain point our education became irrelevant. We said to them, 'We are your children.' We were the kind of American Jews they were trying to produce."[4] The "Call for Change" argued that "to educate women and deny them the opportunity to act from this knowledge is an affront to their intelligence, talent and dignity."[5]

The activists were typical of a growing number of Conservative women: educated in Jewish studies, many at the movement's Ramah summer camps, they were successfully toppling barriers to women in leadership roles within their own congregations. For the next ten years the movement's Jewish Theological Seminary was embroiled in divisive debate concerning the ordination of women.

In 1979, the school's faculty senate tabled the issue of admitting women to the rabbinical school because "the bitter divergence of opinion threatens to inflict irreparable damage." During the debate, the seminary's chancellor, Rabbi Gerson Cohen, said, "I believe it is incumbent upon us to do away with discrimination against women in Judaism." When a successful vote to ordain women finally passed in 1983, an dissenting faculty member said, "We have committed suicide by handing over the whole Conservative movement to the Reform wing."[6]

By the time, a year later, when Amy Eilberg became the first woman to be ordained as a Conservative rabbi,

An Early Fighter for Women's Rights

Jewish women had been active in the abolitionist movement of the nineteenth century, working to bring an end to slavery. They were also among the earliest feminists in the United States. Ernestine Rose, Lillian Wald and Emma Lazarus were well known. Their greatest victory was reached in 1920, when women in the United States finally won the right to vote.

Ernestine Rose was an eloquent fighter for human rights. At an 1852 women's rights convention she proudly proclaimed, "I am an example of the universality of our claims: for not American women only, but a daughter of poor crushed Poland and the downtrodden and persecuted people called Jews . . . I go for emancipation of all kind—white and black, man and woman. Humanity's children are, in my estimation, all one and the same family."

the number of ordained women rabbis in the Reform movement had reached seventy-one. In 1999, over three hundred female Reform rabbis gathered at a convention. One of them said, "Having women in the rabbinate has helped to humanize the profession."[7]

Of the first women rabbis, Dr. Anne Lapidus Lerner, vice-chancellor of the Jewish Theological Seminary, said, "They have to be braver because they are taking the risks; they are the trailblazers."[8] Rabbi Amy Schwartzman, senior rabbi at Temple Rodef Shalom in Falls Church, Virginia, added, "I have one thousand members in my congregation, and none of them had this experience growing up. That contributes to feelings of being different and not being fully accepted."[9]

The Reform movement's seminary, Hebrew Union College, ordained the first American woman rabbi in 1972, Sally Priesand. She was followed two years later by Sandy Eisenberg Sasso, who was ordained by the Reconstructionist Rabbinical College. By the end of the twentieth century, women comprised more than 50 percent of those enrolled in the Reform, Conservative and Reconstructionist seminaries. Others have become cantors in Reform and Conservative temples, and scores of others are active lay leaders within their movements and their congregations. "What began at Hebrew Union College—you can't go back and no one wants to go back—it's part and parcel of American Jewish life," explained Rabbi Kenneth Ehrlich, Dean of the Reform movement's rabbinical school.[10]

In the Orthodox world, increasing numbers of women have become engaged in study and prayer groups as they seek ways to resist the lures of modern secular life and deepen their own Jewish learning. The Israeli direc-

Rabbi Helga Newmark. In May 2000, Newmark was ordained by Hebrew Union College, the first woman Holocaust survivor to become a rabbi. (Associated Press)

tor of one successful program said, "There should never be a point where women stop growing or striving for higher potential."11

Some in the Orthodox community see the increased involvement of women in study groups as a threat to the structure of Jewish family life. "But if you sit down and talk to women interested in prayer groups and talmudic studies," one Orthodox rabbi said, "you discover the vast majority has no intention of bolting from Orthodox life. They're just looking to develop themselves in a profound way."12

The ordination of women marked only one change in the traditional Jewish attitude toward the participation of women in religious life. Like Henrietta Szold, Justice Ruth Bader Ginsburg and Bella Abzug, Susannah Heschel was deeply troubled by the traditional ban on women reciting the *kaddish* prayer. When her father, the renowned scholar Abraham Joshua Heschel, died in 1972, Heschel felt abandoned. "It was the first time I really needed a Jewish community and it failed me." Times have changed. "Never again will a woman not be able to find a place to say *Kaddish* for her father the way I couldn't," Heschel said.13

The Changing Role of Gays in Religious Life

For Jewish gays and lesbians, the quest for equality and recognition began late. Their role in the Jewish world was largely hidden throughout most of the twentieth century because they participated in Jewish life without revealing their sexual orientations. With the successes of the women's movement and the gay rights movement in the 1970s, Jewish gays began coming "out of the closet" and making their presence felt.

Many gays feared rejection and avoided participation in mainstream synagogues. In large cities such as New York and Los Angeles, they joined together to form their own houses of worship. New York's Congregation Beth Simchat Torah was founded in 1973 by people who "rejected the accepted norm that one could not be openly gay and deeply Jewish at the same time." This thriving congregation provides attendees with a wide variety of religious and social services. High Holiday attendance usually exceeds 2,500. The congregation's longtime rabbi, Sharon Kleinbaum, explains that "we have an obligation to do this, offering a place where homosexuals and their families can worship. Critics say that homosexuality destroys the family, but we reconstruct families that have been shattered."[14]

For centuries, the Jewish view on homosexuality was based on strict biblical interpretations. And in spite of Reform Judaism's embrace of liberal viewpoints, no formal recognition of gay rights surfaced until 1977, when its Central Conference of American Rabbis urged states to prohibit discrimination against gay men and women.

With the ordination of the first woman rabbi, pressure began to build for openly gay men and women to be ordained. In 1990, the Reform movement recognized the equality of all members of Reform congregations, regardless of sexual orientation, and it accepted gay and lesbian rabbis. But the Orthodox view was not open to change. Kenneth Hain, president of the Orthodox Rabbinical Council of America, spoke for his movement when he said, "Judaism's laws cannot be abrogated by fiat or majority vote or redesigned to fit a current behavior pattern."

In 1992, the Conservative movement's Jewish Theological Seminary adopted a middle-of-the-road policy that stated, "We will not knowingly admit avowed homosexuals to our rabbinical or cantorial schools, or to the Rabbinical Assembly or the Cantor's Assembly. At the same time, we will not instigate witch-hunts against those who are already members or students."

Toward Equality for All

Ten years after the Reform movement accepted openly gay men and women for ordination, it took a stand on the controversial issue of same-sex marriages. Although not specifically embracing the concept of such marriages, Reform rabbis overwhelmingly approved a resolution giving rabbis the choice of presiding over gay commitment ceremonies. The wording of the official resolution, adopted in 2000, states that "the relationship of a Jewish, same-gender couple is worthy of affirmation through appropriate Jewish ritual."

Rabbi Eric Yoffie, head of the Union of American Hebrew Congregations, said that "loving, permanent homosexual relationships, once difficult to conceive, are now recognized as an indisputable reality . . . Reform Jews [need to] create an inclusive spiritual home for all those who seek the solace of our sanctuaries." Rabbi Shira Stern of the Women's Rabbinic Network said, "This is not a women's issue, or a gay or lesbian issue. This is a human rights issue. . . ."

Coming of Age Politically:
The Selection of Joseph Lieberman

*"Politically,
we've come out
of the closet."*

HON. STUART
EIZENSTAT

I n 1937, a public opinion poll asked Americans if they would vote for a Jewish candidate for president. Forty-six percent answered yes. Response to the same question in 1999 was 92 percent. Still, when in 2000 Al Gore picked Senator Joseph Lieberman as his running mate for vice president, it was viewed as a risky political move. Before Lieberman's selection, even the chairman of the Democratic National Committee, Ed Rendell, who is himself Jewish, said, "I don't think anyone can calculate the effect of having a Jew on the ticket. If Mr. Lieberman were Episcopalian it would be a slam dunk." Even after a century of increasing acceptance of Jews in the United States, Jews could not fully dismiss old fears.

Until this time, the idea of a Jewish president or vice president had been only a dream for Jews. Yet parents had always instilled in their children the belief that in America, anything is possible. Even the realities of day-to-day discrimination could not dim the hope that some-day all barriers to complete Jewish involvement in

Senator Joseph Lieberman. As the Democratic Party's nominee for vice president in 2000, Senator Lieberman became the first Jew ever to run for the second highest elective office in the United States. *(Associated Press)*

American life would eventually fall. The nomination of Joseph Lieberman was a turning point for Jews and for the country.

Senator Lieberman is not just Jewish, he is an observant modern Orthodox Jew. Prior to his nomination, the most visibly active Jews in American political life had been either secular or connected with the more liberal branches of Judaism. They kept a low profile regarding their personal religious practices. Few expected that the first Jewish candidate for the second highest position in the land would be Orthodox.

When his name was announced as the vice presidential choice of the Democratic Party in 2000, much was made of his religion. The attention was in sharp contrast to a presidential appointment just seven years earlier.

Ruth Bader Ginsburg on the Bench

On August 10, 1993, Ruth Bader Ginsburg was sworn in as an associate justice of the United States Supreme Court. She was not the first Jew or even the first woman appointed to the court. What made this event remarkable was the routine manner in which the American public treated her nomination and

Is America a Great Country or What?

Joseph Lieberman was born in Stamford, Connecticut, to poor, hard-working parents. He graduated from Yale College in 1964 and Yale Law School in 1967. After serving in the state legislature for ten years, he was elected attorney general of Connecticut. In 1988, he was elected to the United States Senate, where he quickly became respected for his integrity and highly ethical behavior. As an observant Jew, he did not work on Saturday, but when it was necessary for him to cast a vote on a Saturday, he walked several miles from his home to the Capitol.

After losing with Al Gore in the close presidential election of 2000, he spoke of his selection as the Democratic Party candidate for vice president. "I began by asking: Is America a great country or what? Last night, we ended that remarkable journey in a disappointing way. But nevertheless, I want to answer my question this morning by declaring: Yes, America is a great country."

He continued, " . . . in selecting me, a Jewish American, to be his running mate, Vice President Gore did what no presidential candidate before him had done . . . The absence of bigotry in this campaign . . . should, I think, encourage every parent in this country to dream the biggest dreams for each and every one of their children. Anything is possible in America."

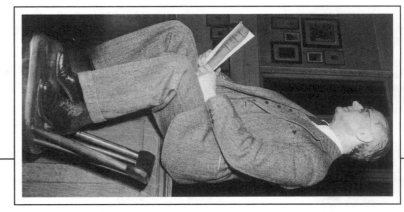

Supreme Court Justice Felix Frankfurter, teaching at Harvard Law School. Justice Frankfurter was born in Austria in 1882, and his family came to the United States twelve years later. He graduated from Harvard Law School, where he served as editor of the *Law Review* there. In 1939, President Franklin Roosevelt appointed him to the Supreme Court. Frankfurter died in 1965. *(Library of Congress)*

Senate confirmation. The fact that she was Jewish—the first Jewish woman appointed to the Court—was not an impediment to her nomination and confirmation.

Ruth Bader was born on March 15, 1933, in Brooklyn, New York. As a child, she enjoyed reading and writing and was active in school activities. Sixty years later she wrote, "World War II raged on during my grade school years. Jews fortunate enough to be in the United States during those years could hardly avoid identifying themselves with the cause of the Jewish people."

The day before her high school graduation in 1950, Ruth's mother died. Throughout her life Ruth was an admirer of Henrietta Szold. Similar experiences upon the death of a parent affected both Szold's and Ginsburg's outlooks on the role of women in Judaism. "I couldn't say *Kaddish* [prayer for the dead] when my mother died," Ruth Bader Ginsburg later said. "I remember thinking then that [the Jewish law] was wrong." Traditional Jewish law prohibited women from reciting the prayer.

Ruth Bader met her husband, Martin Ginsburg, at law school, where she was one of nine women in a class of over five hundred students. Even as a law school student and later as a lawyer she experienced discrimination—not as a Jew, but as a woman. For example, at a dinner honoring the women students, the dean turned to each of them in turn to ask what she was doing at the law school occupying a seat that could have been filled by a man.

After graduating at the top of her class from Columbia University Law School in 1959, Ginsburg experienced the rejection common to women of her time. As she later recounted, "Not a single law firm in the entire city of New York bid for my employment." She became a professor of law at Rutgers Law School and a founder of the American Civil Liberties Union (ACLU) Women's Rights Project, fighting against sex discrimination. In 1980, President Jimmy Carter appointed her to the United States Court of Appeals for the District of Columbia.

She served for thirteen years on the court of appeals before being appointed to the Supreme Court by President Clinton in 1993. "I never thought of the possibility of being a judge," she said when she became an associate justice of the Supreme Court. "When I got out

Campaign poster for Congresswoman Bella Abzug. She was a well-known civil rights attorney when she ran for Congress at the age of fifty. Abzug served three terms in the House of Representatives, where she fought for women's rights and in opposition to the Vietnam War. *(Library of Congress)*

Louis D. Brandeis's Earlier Fight for Confirmation

The nomination and confirmation of Justice Ruth Bader Ginsburg was uneventful in contrast to the confirmation in 1916 of Louis D. Brandeis, the first Jewish member of the Supreme Court. Brandeis, an early leader of American Zionism, had been a well-known lawyer active in the labor and civil rights movements. His work on behalf of social justice brought him to national

of law school and began to teach, women were only 3 percent of my students. This is a great time in my life."

During the 1950s and 1960s, Jewish attorneys worked closely with civil rights organizations to battle discrimination. When asked why Jews were so concerned with civil rights questions, an earlier Jewish Supreme Court Justice, Felix Frankfurter, responded, "One who belongs to the most vilified and persecuted minority in history is not likely to be insensitive to the freedoms guaranteed by the Constitution." When the American Bar Association presented Justice Ginsburg with its coveted Thurgood Marshall Award, named for the first African-American Supreme Court Justice, Ginsburg was eloquent in her acceptance:

My advocacy, of course, did not begin to compare with Thurgood Marshall's. My life was never in danger, and the ACLU litigation I superintended was never the only show in town . . . But of one thing there is no doubt. I gained courage and inspiration from Marshall's example.

prominence. Although he had grown up in Louisville, Kentucky, "free from Jewish contacts or traditions," he became a leader of the Zionist movement in the United States. "To be good Americans," Brandeis said, "We must be better Jews, and to be better Jews, we must become Zionists." When President Woodrow Wilson nominated him to the Supreme Court in 1916, the president "did not see any contradiction between a special humanitarian interest in the Jews of Palestine and American interests."

Others, however, felt threatened. Never before had there been a Jew in such a highly visible and important government position. Pressed to withdraw the nomination, President Wilson held fast. The headline in the *New York Sun* declared, "HE'S THE FIRST JEW EVER PICKED FOR THE BENCH." Debate on his confirmation dragged along for four months in the United States Senate. Not so subtly, some of the opposition to the nomination centered on the candidate's religious background. A chief opponent of Brandeis was Senator Henry Cabot Lodge of Massachusetts. In a letter marked personal and confidential, Lodge wrote a friend, "If it were not that Brandeis was a Jew, and a German Jew, he would never have been appointed."[1]

When Senate confirmation hearings began, the list of opponents to Brandeis read like a "who's who" of business, academia and banking, including the president of Harvard University. Letters and telegrams on both sides of the candidacy poured into Washington. A rabbi wrote, "Your nomination of Mr. Louis D. Brandeis was received with great joy and enthusiasm." In contrast, a doctor commented that he was ". . . much surprised to learn that you have recommended a Hebrew for the Supreme Bench. I feel if you knew the unfavorable comments that the writer has listened to in the social clubs and the public places you would reconsider the matter."[2]

Remarks on the candidate's Judaism and anti-Semitic newspaper cartoons and jokes spread across the country. The dean of the Boston University Law School related the following joke to former president William Howard Taft. "What is the difference between William H. Taft and Louis D. Brandeis? Why, the former is distinguished in jurisprudence and the latter in Jewish prudence."[3]

A Boston stockbroker wrote to Massachusetts Senator David Walsh:

The fact that a slimy fellow of this kind . . . together with his Jewish instinct, can almost land in the cabinet, and probably on the bench of the Supreme Court of the United States, should teach an object lesson to men who believe that for future generations manhood should be the test . . . rather than showing that shysters can reach the goal.[4]

The outcry against Brandeis was not just because of prevailing anti-Semitic sentiment; many opposed his advocacy of worker's rights. But in spite of the heated arguments against him, Brandeis was ultimately confirmed. The *Los Angeles Morning Tribune* commented that "the appointment of Louis D. Brandeis gives the Supreme Court of the United States its first thorough-

Justice Cardozo

In 1932, President Herbert Hoover appointed Benjamin Cardozo to the Supreme Court. Cardozo, the second Jewish member of the Court, was descended from an old Sephardic family. But his elite status did not exclude him from personally experiencing the anti-Semitism of the time. In the 1928 presidential election, he publicly supported Hoover's Democratic opponent, writing that in the Republican Party "will be found all the narrow-minded bigots, all the Jew haters, all those who would make of the United States an exclusively Protestant government. . . ."

going radical . . . [who] has been the aggressive champion of the rights of the plain people."[5]

When Justice Brandeis retired in 1939, President Franklin Roosevelt appointed Felix Frankfurter to the court in his place. The tradition of a "Jewish seat" on the Supreme Court continued through 1969. President Kennedy appointed his secretary of labor, Arthur Goldberg, to the seat in 1962. When in 1965 Goldberg resigned at the personal of request of President Lyndon Johnson to become United States ambassador to the United Nations, Johnson appointed Abe Fortas to the Court. From 1916 until Fortas's resignation in 1969, there had always been at least one Jewish associate justice on the Supreme Court.

But after that there were no Jews on the Supreme Court until Ruth Bader Ginsburg's appointment in 1993. By then, the idea of a "Jewish seat" on the Supreme Court had disappeared. Candidates were selected on their abilities, without regard to their religion.

A Growing Presence
on the Political Scene

In the early years of the United States, when the Jewish population was very small, a number of American Jews did indeed get elected to local, state, and national offices. But getting there wasn't easy; some states barred Jews from elected positions. Beginning in 1797, Jewish citizens of Maryland regularly petitioned their legislature for equal status. In 1824, the "Jew Bill" finally passed, and two years later two Jews were elected to the Baltimore City Council. Throughout the nineteenth century, Jews were to be numbered among the

President Gerald Ford and his advisor Max Fisher. Fisher was an important fundraiser for the Republican Party. Presidents Richard Nixon and Gerald Ford both relied on him for advice on Jewish political matters, especially the United States' relations with Israel. *(Gerald R. Ford Library)*

country's mayors, governors, and members of Congress. One of the most notable office holders was Judah Benjamin, who, prior to the Civil War, abandoned his seat in the United States Senate to become secretary of state for the Confederacy.

At the beginning of the twentieth century, when two million Russian Jews emigrated to America, the first Jew was appointed to the president's cabinet. Theodore Roosevelt selected Oscar Straus to serve as his secretary of labor. Roosevelt said he wanted "to show Russia and some other countries what we think of Jews in this country."[6]

Perhaps it was the fear of anti-Semitism or the old "sha-sha" syndrome (see chapter two) that kept many Jews from seeking elected office during most of the twentieth century. That reluctance did not, however, preclude them from some involvement in American political life. There were always a few Jewish congressmen during the 1920s, 30s and 40s. Most of them came from heavily Jewish districts.

Early in the century in New York, Jewish voters could be counted on to support the political organization established by earlier immigrants. The 1914 election of Meyer London to Congress, representing New York's Lower East Side, changed all this. London's victory—a Jew voted into office by, essentially, Jews—broke the Jewish population's dependence on others and symbolized the desire of the recent immigrants to get involved in the American political process on their own terms. London was a Socialist, a Yiddish-speaking labor activist who understood the needs and dreams of his working-class constituents.

President Ronald Reagan addressing a convention of the United Jewish Appeal. Although President Reagan felt a strong personal attachment to Israel, his administration was embroiled in nearly constant argument with Israeli leaders over the possibility of peace with the Palestinians. *(Ronald Reagan Library)*

At the highest level of government, there were always certain people who, because of their reputations and ties to elected officials, could be counted on to represent Jewish interests. This was a throwback to the European model of the *shtadlan* or court Jew, who had influence with a country's ruler. Rabbi Stephen S. Wise was a confidant to President Franklin Roosevelt. Eddie Jacobson is credited with persuading his close friend President Harry Truman to recognize the fledgling State of Israel in 1948. Max Fisher, a Republican fundraiser, advised Presidents Richard Nixon and Gerald Ford on Jewish issues.

Through the 1970s, while Jews could be found on congressional staffs, in appointed positions and as political fundraisers, few actively sought out elective office. During that time, there were only two Jewish senators: Jacob Javits of New York and Abraham Ribicoff of Connecticut. When Barry Goldwater, whose father was born Jewish, became the Republican candidate for president in 1964, humorist Harry Golden, anticipating a Goldwater victory, wrote, "I always knew the first Jewish president would be an Episcopalian."

By the 1990s, Jewish participation in American political life was no longer a curiosity. In the 1996 campaign for the U.S. Senate in Minnesota, the Democrat, Paul Wellstone, narrowly defeated the Republican incumbent, Rudy Boschwitz. Both were Jewish, and one of the campaign issues in a state with a tiny Jewish population was the "superior" Jewishness of one candidate over the other. After the 1998 election, there were eleven Jewish members in the United States Senate, enough to com-

Jewish Community Center, Pittsburgh, Pennsylvania. Jewish houses of worship and community centers are highly visible in cities around the country. The clock on the tower of Pittsburgh's Jewish Community Center proudly displays Hebrew letters. *(Rauh Archives, Historical Society of Western Pennsylvania)*

prise a minyan, a quorum to hold Jewish religious services. While both senators from California and Wisconsin were Jewish, other Jewish senators represented states with few Jewish residents. There were twenty-three Jewish members in the House of Representatives. One of the new members was Congresswoman Shelley Berkley from Las Vegas, Nevada. "It's very important to me," she said, "to be a Jew, first and foremost. I didn't want to be someone in politics who happens to be a Jew."[7]

While Jews have held a wide variety of state and national elective offices, the presidency still seemed out of reach in the 1990s. When Senator Arlen Specter of Pennsylvania became a candidate for the 1996 Republican nomination for president, he came face to face with lingering anti-Semitism. "I'm not totally unused to it," Specter said. "It's always been a little bit

Religious Equality in Practice

Senator Joseph Lieberman of Connecticut is a devout Orthodox Jew who observes the Sabbath and the rules of kashrut. Speaking at the annual National Prayer Breakfast in Washington on February 3, 2000, he alluded to the discomfort many Jews experienced when confronted by perceived Christian customs. "When I was first invited years ago to the Senate Prayer Breakfast," he told the gathering, which included President Clinton and members of Congress, "I found a lot of excuses not to go . . . But some excuses were not so good—like my apprehension that the Senate Prayer Breakfast was really a Christian breakfast and that, because I am Jewish, I might feel awkward or my presence might inhibit my Christian friends in their expressions of faith. I was wrong on both counts."[8]

Quiet No More

different being Jewish." His candidacy did not go far but it did establish the precedent of a qualified Jewish contender for the presidency. In some ways, his candidacy could be likened to the 1928 unsuccessful presidential campaign of New York Governor Al Smith. Smith was a Roman Catholic and no one of his religious background had ever reached the White House. But less than thirty years later, another Roman Catholic, John F. Kennedy, was elected president of the United States.

By the end of the twentieth century, Jews could be found in a variety of governmental positions. Stuart Eizenstat served as an aide to President Jimmy Carter and held a number of ranking positions during the two administrations of President Bill Clinton. Unlike his Jewish predecessors, Eizenstat was always forthcoming about his strong connections to Judaism.

Rabbi Irving "Yitz" Greenberg explained, "The previous generation was extremely cautious, if not self-denying, as Jews." Eizenstat, according to Rabbi Greenberg, had a deep "inner commitment and security to be a Jew not afraid to deal with the Jewish agenda positively."[9]

In 1997, Eizenstat told a gathering of Jewish political leaders, "What we've seen over the past twenty or twenty-five years is Jews coming of age, in a political sense. We've become much more vocal, not just as an outside interest group, but by integrating into the system."[10] At one time, Jewish involvement in politics centered largely on Israel. Today, there is a Jewish presence on many issues, domestic and international. Gone is a unified Jewish view on many issues, and members of Congress now realize that there are many different perspectives within the Jewish community.

In 1994, President Clinton nominated a second Jew to the Supreme Court: Stephen Breyer. As with Ginsburg, Breyer's Senate confirmation was remarkable

Jews and the Democratic Party

There is a traditional Jewish connection to the Democratic Party. Although there have been notable exceptions, Jewish voters tend to be more liberal politically than their non-Jewish neighbors. Even as economic conditions improved, Jews have remained loyal Democrats, unlike other ethnic groups that shifted to the Republican Party as they became wealthier.

Earl Raab, a sociologist, wrote that "if you scratch an American Jew, you will find, as ever, a Democratic voter . . . but if you scratch somewhat deeper, you will not always find a liberal." While some of the economic policies of the Republican Party may be appealing to some, American Jews are nervous about many Christian Fundamentalist and right-wing causes favored by the party. Jews have long championed civil rights, gun control legislation, abortion rights and a strict separation of church and state. These issues make them feel more comfortable within the Democratic Party.

because of its routineness. Speaking at graduation exercises at Stanford University in 1997, Justice Breyer reflected on the changes that had occurred during the last century:

When my father was at Stanford, he could not join any of the social organizations because he was Jewish . . . Indeed I can remember, as a child, my mother thinking of going to lunch at a downtown San Francisco hotel with a friend of hers who was African-American, and their discussing whether they would be served. When my colleagues, Justices Sandra Day O'Connor and Ruth Bader Ginsburg, graduated from law school, they had trouble finding jobs—because they were women. So did Senator [Dianne] Feinstein. The world has changed . . . I think it is very important to remember that those changes did not occur magically—that they represented individual, and collective, pioneering efforts. We need to remember those efforts, both because so many of us now benefit from them and because there is so much still to be done. You still can choose to be a pioneer.

The Barriers Fall

By the end of the twentieth century, Jews served as presidents of several major universities, including Harvard, Yale, Princeton and Dartmouth. Jews served in presidential cabinets as secretaries of state, labor, treasury, commerce and agriculture. They served as chairman of the Federal Reserve Bank, director of the

Central Intelligence Agency, and as the Navy chief of staff. In business, Jews led major corporations in positions that had been closed to them for decades.

In many ways, the appointment of Ruth Bader Ginsburg to the Supreme Court was a historic moment in political history. For too long, as Jews quietly rose to prominence in government service, some people kept a count. Jewish leaders knew this, and it made them fear that awareness of the numbers could reinforce anti-Semitic claims that Jews controlled the American government. But finally, by the end of the twentieth century, these leaders were comfortable enough to publicly bask in the glow of political success. The nomination of Joseph Lieberman in 2000 finally put to rest the belief that a Jew—particularly an observant Jew—could not take part in national political life. As to the future? The possibilities are endless.

CHAPTER 11

Facing the Future: Where Are We? Where Are We Headed?

"We have a system of living and values that the world needs. But first we must be a light unto the Jews. Let's start with our kids."

YOSEF I. ABRAMOWITZ

A 1970s advertising jingle that targeted women proclaimed, "You've come a long way, baby." During the preceding one hundred years, dramatic progress had occurred in the United States socially, economically and politically. The Jews of America were not immune. At the beginning of the twentieth century, most of them were strangers in a new land—recent immigrants from oppression and poverty in Eastern Europe. In one century, American Jews had gone from marginalization to sophistication, from observers of American culture to creators of it.

Indeed, the Jewish experience is now integrated into everyday American life on many levels. Americans are eating bagels and often using Yiddish words. They buy books by Jewish authors, watch television programs featuring Jewish stars, listen to music written and performed by Jews and vote for Jewish politicians. By the close of the twentieth century, Jews were fully involved in all aspects of American life.

The End of
Institutional Anti-Semitism

O n a personal level, the advances made by American Jews are equally remarkable. Today, they earn higher incomes than most other Americans. Six out of ten Jewish adults are college graduates. Jews are no longer excluded from jobs, clubs or schools because of their religion.

The overt anti-Semitism of the first half of the century has given way to general acceptance and inclusion. Congressman Barney Frank, Jewish and gay, reflected on this change in an article for the Wilstein Institute:

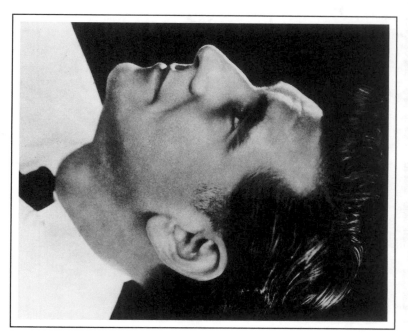

Composer Leonard Bernstein. Born in Lawrence, Massachusetts, in 1918, Bernstein was appointed assistant conductor of the New York Philharmonic Orchestra in 1943 and became music director there in 1958. His many recordings of classical music and his conducting roles throughout the world made him famous. Bernstein was an important composer as well, often drawing on Jewish themes. He also contributed to the musical theater, collaborating on such well-known plays as *On the Town* and *West Side Story*. (*Library of Congress*)

We no longer need law firms composed primarily of Jewish partners, as refuges for bright Jewish lawyers denied a chance to practice elsewhere. Thirty years ago, partner lists on law firm letterheads were much more religiously and ethnically homogenous than today's polyglot lists. Doctors practicing medicine in hospitals, professors becoming presidents of Ivy League institutions—the list is a long one for areas in our national life where Jewish Americans once faced slammed doors and [could] not walk regularly through open ones.[1]

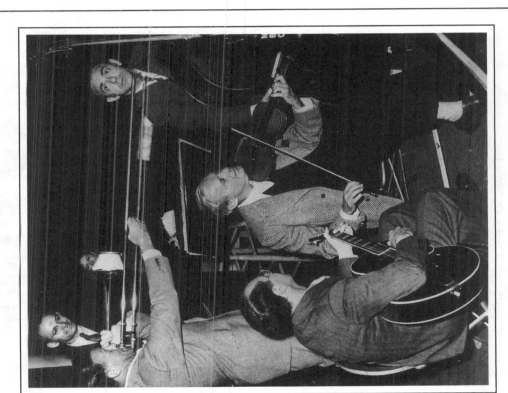

"Jam session" with four leading Jewish entertainers of the 1930s and 40s: Groucho Marx on guitar, George Burns on trombone, Jack Benny on violin and Eddie Cantor on bass. (Special Collections Department, University Research Library, UCLA)

184

Jerry Seinfeld.
Seinfeld **was one of
the most popular
sitcoms on television
during the 1990s.
Seinfeld was Jewish,
and he incorporated
obvious Jewish humor
in the show.**
(Associated Press)

Yet anti-Semitism still exists. In 2001, a United Nations Conference on racism turned into an unrestricted attack on Israel, Judaism and Zionism. Later that year, in the immediate aftermath of the terrorist attack on the World Trade Center in New York, some anti-Semites were quick to cry "It's all the Jews' fault." Nonetheless, with the exception of isolated but sometimes violent incidents, Jews are more secure and accepted than at any time in history. Congressman Frank described his own political journey:

When I began to think of politics as a profession in the 1960's, one of the major things I had to take into account in making my own plans was the severe limitations facing me or any other Jewish candidate for public office. Jewish candidates rarely won outside of constituencies with large Jewish populations. We tended to opt during most of our life in America for appointed positions, for advisory roles. Many of us felt constrained by fear of anti-Semitism from taking too prominent a position, especially by seeking elective office, and when we tried, we often failed because of prejudice . . . I would not have believed twenty years ago that there would be four Jewish senators from California and Wisconsin, all elected with very little indication of effective anti-Semitism.[2]

Popular bread advertisement in the 1960s. This ad for Levy's rye bread was a first in reaching non-Jewish shoppers. Since then, ads for bagels, kosher chickens and kosher hot dogs have brought Jewish foods into the American mainstream. (Library of Congress)

You don't have to be Jewish

to love Levy's
real Jewish Rye

Insecurity and Concern

When Joseph Lieberman was nominated as the Democratic candidate for vice president in 2000, some Jews nervously anticipated increased anti-Semitism. Others saw the nomination as a sign that previous barriers to Jews had largely fallen. The candidate himself could only marvel, "What a great country this is."

I n spite of this progress, American Jews, as a group, still feel insecure about themselves and their future. They are, after all, a shrinking minority, from a high of 4 percent of the American population in 1950 to somewhere around 2.7 percent in 2000, Jews are not numerically significant. Some experts estimate that within the next few decades the Muslim population in the United States will exceed that of the Jews. Although the advances made by Jews ally them more to the mainstream than to the margins of American life, they still see themselves as a vulnerable minority. Their high profile has given them such exposure that many Americans, when asked to guess the percentage of Jews in the United States, frequently respond with answers of 40 and 50 percent!

As Jews became a driving force in the building of the United States, they also creat-

Where Do American Jews Live?

In 1900, most American Jews lived in large cities—New York, Chicago, Boston. By 2000, the Jewish population shifted to the suburbs. While the Northeast held over 40 percent of the American Jewish population, 21 percent lived in the South, 21 percent in the West and 12 percent in the Midwest.

New York State had the highest percentage: 9.1 percent, followed by New Jersey: 5.8 percent, the District of Columbia: 4.8 percent, Massachusetts: 4.5 percent, and Florida: 4.3 percent.[3]

ed a uniquely American form of Jewish community and religion. Many compared the Jewish experience in this country with the Golden Age of Jews in Spain centuries earlier. Yet, as in Spain, all was not perfect. In spite of many advances, American Jews have become increasingly concerned about their relationship with Israel, and the family and communal issues of intermarriage, assimilation, declining numbers and loss of Jewish literacy.

Israel

For most of the twentieth century, Israel was the centerpoint of American Jewish life. Over centuries, Jews have concluded the Passover seder and the Yom Kippur service with the words, "next year in Jerusalem." While their ancestors could only dream of a return to Zion, the modern State of Israel is today alive and robust in spite of continuing concern for its security. Although Israel remains important for American Jews, a reordering of priorities has dampened its centrality.

At the beginning of the twentieth century, the majority of the world's Jewish population lived in Eastern Europe. Following the Holocaust and the establishment of the State of Israel, those numbers decreased dramatically. While sizable Jewish populations can today be found in countries such as Russia, France and Argentina,

The Future Jewish Population

The worldwide Jewish population is expected to grow from 13.1 million in 2000 to 13.8 million by 2020, 14 million in 2030 and 15 million in 2080.

Israel's Jewish population is expected to double by 2080.

In the United States, the Jewish population is expected to drop from 5.7 million in 2000 to 5.6 million in 2020, to 4.7 million in 2050 and 3.8 million in 2080.[4]

their futures are uncertain. Within the next few decades, it is expected that the largest numbers of the world's Jews will be found nearly equally divided between two countries—Israel and the United States. This dramatic shift will create new problems and new opportunities.

Family and Community

Jews are increasingly concerned with continuity and the state of Jewish education. Barry Schrage, President of Boston's Combined Jewish Philanthropies, explained:

For the first twenty years following the '67 war, Israel became the banner, the symbol, and the central story of what bound Jews together. The Jewish community is now attempting to balance that with the development of stronger community life. It's not that we don't love Israel as much, but Israel has become so strong, there may be less need.[5]

Suburban Filene's department store, Peabody, Massachusetts. The United States' best-known department stores were founded by German Jewish immigrants in the mid-nineteenth century. Over several decades, their little stores, or peddler's packs, grew into important retail businesses such as Filene's, Macy's, Gimbels, Hechts and Lazarus. *(Library of Congress)*

Macy's famous New York headquarters. By 1931, when this photograph was taken, Macy's had been become the country's best-known department store. *(Library of Congress)*

How will Jewish community life change in the twenty-first century? A new focus will be on nurturing the religious, cultural and social life of Jewish families. A 1992 report by the American Jewish Committee, "The High Cost of Jewish Living," revealed that the average Jewish family was priced out of many Jewish institutions. The massive fundraising campaigns of Jewish Federations will more actively support Jewish day schools, summer camps and synagogue activities. For in the end, the future of Jewish life in the United States depends on the vitality and commitment of its families.

Jonathan Woocher, executive director of the Jewish Education Service of America, said, "Jewish life cannot be about fighting assimilation: it has to be about something else. Being Jewish today means a lot of different things. There is this incredible diversity of how Jews define, practice, believe."[6] The question Jews continue to face is how best to meld the freedoms of America with their religious and cultural heritage.

Notes

Chapter One

1. Neil Gilman, *Conservative Judaism* (New York: Behrman House, 1993), 13.

2. *Commentary* 110 (May 1999): 107.

3. From the Preamble of the Constitution of the National Council of Young Israel.

4. *Jewish Telegraphic Agency Bulletin* (October 12, 1999).

Chapter Two

1. "Jews of New York," *Review of Reviews* 13 (1896): 59.

2. *New York Evening Journal* (November 28, 1909).

3. *New York Call* (November 23, 1909). Quoted in Louis Stein, *Out of the Sweatshop* (New York: Quadrangle, 1977), 69–70.

4. Mary van Kleeck, *Charities and Commons* 17 (July 1909): 16.

5. *The New York Times* (March 26, 1911): 1.

6. Leon Stein, *The Triangle Fire* (New York: Lippincott, 1962), 148.

7. Zilphia Horton Folk Music Collection, Tennessee State Library and Archives, Nashville, Tenn.

Chapter Three

1. Arthur A. Goren, ed. *Dissenter in Zion* (Cambridge: Harvard University Press, 1982), 18.

2. Ibid., 100.

3. Ibid., 101.

4. Ibid., 99.

5. Ibid., 100.

6. Ibid., 67.

7. Ibid., 251.

8. Ibid., 250.

9. Philip Bernstein, *To Dwell in Unity: The Jewish Federation Movement in America Since 1960* (Philadelphia: The Jewish Publication Society, 1983), 4.

Chapter Four

1. Norman H. Finkelstein, *Heeding the Call: Jewish Voices in America's Civil Rights Struggle* (Philadelphia: The Jewish Publication Society, 1997), 21.

2. Ibid., 51.

3. New York *Newsday* (November 25, 1998): B6.

4. Ibid., B6.

5. Harry Golden, *The Lynching of Leo Frank* (New York: Cassell, 1966), 227.

6. Ibid., 229.

7. Leonard Dinnerstein, *The Leo Frank Case* (New York: Columbia University Press, 1968), 53.

8. *Atlanta Journal* (March 10,1914): 8.

9. Golden, *Lynching of Leo Frank*, 358.

10. Dinnerstein, *Leo Frank Case*, 62.

11. Leonard Dinnerstein, "The Fate of Leo Frank," *American Heritage* (October 1996): 98.

12. *Dearborn Independent* (March 12, 1921).

13. Ibid., November 26, 1921.

14. Ibid., March 19, 1921.

15. Ibid., November 26, 1921.

16. *San Francisco Examiner* (November 13, 1991).

17. Golden, *Lynching of Leo Frank*, 309.

Chapter Five

1. *Time* (May 16, 1988).

2. George Jessel, October 26, 1950.

3. Nomi Morris, "Jews in Tinseltown," *Macleans* 3 (March 9, 1998): 70.

4. Michael Rogan, *Jewish Bulletin of Northern California* (October 2, 1998).

5. *Los Angeles Times* (March 23, 1998).

6. *The Republican* 5 (January 1912): 11.

7. Don L. F. Nilson, "Humorous Contemporary Jewish-American Authors: An Overview of The Criticism," *Melus* 21 (winter 1996): 71.

8. Ibid., 72.

9. Ivy Garlitz, "Evocations in Popular Culture: The Multiple Identities of Superman," (unpublished speech at the Seventh Annual Comic Arts Conference, San Diego, August 1999): 2.

10. Michael Granberry, "One of Major League Baseball's Few Jewish Players Talks About How Faith Affect Life On the Field," *Dallas Morning News* (June 7, 2000).

11. *Jewish News of Greater Phoenix* (January 8, 1999).

Chapter Six

1. From *The Tageblatt* (November 10, 1914). Quoted in Mordecai Soltes, *The Yiddish Press* (New York: Columbia University Teacher's College, 1925).

2. Joan Dash, *Summoned To Jerusalem* (New York: Harper, 1979), 25.

3. Milton Meltzer, *Starting From Home* (New York: Viking, 1988), 25.

4. From *The Day* (September 14, 1922). Quoted in Soltes, *Yiddish Press.*

5. Hutchins Hapgood, *The Spirit of the Ghetto*, ed. Moses Rischin (Cambridge, Massachusetts: Belknap Press, 1967), 24.

6. Peter Beinart, "Education and Rise of Jewish Schools," *Atlantic Monthly* 2 (October 1999): 21.

7. *Jewish Advocate* (October 13, 1927).

8. Arthur A. Goren, *New York Jews and the Quest for Community* (New York: Columbia University Press, 1970), 99.

9. Marvin Schick, *A Census of Jewish Day School in the United States,* (New York: Avi Chai Foundation, 2000). Courtesy of the Avi Chai Foundation.

10. Kristin Holmes, *Philadelphia Inquirer* (September 20, 1998): B01.

Chapter Seven

1. Quoted in Norman H. Finkelstein, *Heeding the Call: The Life of Edward R. Murrow* (New York: Clarion, 1997), 102–103.

2. Stephen S. Wise, *The Challenging Years: The Autobiography of Stephen S. Wise* (New York: Putnam, 1949).

3. Quoted in E. Thomas Wood and Stanislaw M. Jankowski, *How One Man Tried to Stop the Holocaust* (New York: Wiley, 1994).

4. *The New York Times* (March 21, 1933).

5. Ibid., (March 28, 1933).

6. Ibid., (July 21, 1935).

7. Finkelstein, *Heeding the Call*, 45.

8. Letter from John J. McCloy to John W. Pehle, War Refugee Board, November 18, 1944.

9. Deborah Dash Moore, "Jewish GI's and the Creation of the Judeo-Christian Tradition," *Religion and American Culture* 8 (winter 1998): s1.

10. Arnold Jacob Wolf, "The Shoah in America," *Judaism: A Quarterly of Jewish Life and Thought* 48 (fall 1999): 490.

11. Marilyn Henry, "AJC Survey," *Jerusalem Post* (March 3, 1998).

12. *JTA Bulletin* (March 15, 2000).

Chapter Eight

1. Myer Feldman, Oral History, John F. Kennedy Library, August 28, 1967.

2. John Slawson, AJC Oral History, Quoted in *American Jewish History* 86 (March 1998): 27.

3. Statistic from the Government of Israel.

4. *Washington Post* (February 20, 1994): A39.

5. "Jews in the United States and Israel Differ on Palestinian State," *Los Angeles Times* (April 19, 1998).

6. Samuel Heilman, "Separated But Not Divorced," *Society* 8 (May-June 1999): 8.

7. *International Herald Tribune* (April 29, 1998).

8. "Young Adults Go To Israel," *JTA Bulletin* (January 12, 1994).

Chapter Nine

1. *Jerusalem Post* (February 15, 1998): 4.
2. Letter from Bella Abzug to Temple Shalom Senior Youth Group, March 13, 1974, Bella Abzug Papers, Columbia University. Quoted in Joyce Antler, *The Journey Home* (New York: Schocken Books, 1997), 269.
3. Quoted in Antler, *Journey Home*, 278–279.
4. *Los Angeles Times* (April 21, 1998): A1.
5. Freedman, Samuel, *Jew vs. Jew* (New York: Simon and Schuster, 2000), 120.
6. *Time* (November 7, 1983): 83.
7. *Minnesota Women's Press* (April 28, 1999).
8. Jill Davidson Sklar, "A Woman's Touch," *Atlanta Jewish Times* (May 1, 1998).
9. Julie Irwin, "Women Rabbis Less Rare," *Cincinnati Enquirer* (August 23, 1998).
10. Ibid.
11. *Hadassah* (October 1997).
12. "Women Help Reshape Jewish Life," *Los Angeles Times* (April 2, 1998).
13. Ibid., 1.
14. Antler, *Journey Home*, 304.

Chapter Ten

1. Quoted in A. L. Todd, *Justice on Trial* (New York: McGraw-Hill, 1964), 85.
2. Ibid., 139.
3. Ibid., 217.
4. Ibid., 143.
5. Ibid., 175.
6. Quoted in Rufus Learsi, *The Jews in America* (New York: Ktav, 1954), 202.
7. Daniel Kurtzman, "Jewish Novices on Capitol Hill Carry Forth Old Political Tradition," *JTA Bulletin* (March 17, 2000).
8. Remarks of Senator Joseph Lieberman, February 3, 2000.
9. Daniel Kurtzman, "Mix of Judaism, Politics Guides Eizenstat in Shaping US Policy," *JTA Bulletin* (June 10, 1999).
10. James D. Besser, "Jews Growing as a Visible Political Force in Washington," *Jewish Bulletin of Northern California* (January 24, 1997).

Chapter Eleven

1. Quoted in Murray Friedman, "Are American Jews Moving to the Right?" *Commentary* (April 2000): 50.

2. Barney Frank, "Pushing Back the Boundaries of Anti-Semitism," in *At the Crossroads* (Brookline, Massachusetts: The Wilstein Institute, 1995).

3. Ibid.

4. From "Jewish Population in the United States, 1999," in *American Jewish Yearbook, 2000* (New York: American Jewish Committee, 2000).

5. From "Projecting the Jewish Future: Population Projections, 2000–2080," in *American Jewish Yearbook 2000* (New York: American Jewish Committee, 2000).

6. Michael Paulson, "From Patron to Partner, *Boston Globe* (July 30, 2000): F01.

7. *The Miami Herald* (January 17, 2000): 3B.

Timeline

1654   First Jewish settlers arrive in New Amsterdam

1824   Passage of Maryland's "Jew Bill" granting Jews the right to hold elective office

1848   Arrival of large numbers of Jews from Germany. Growth of Reform Judaism in America

1881   Beginning of massive Jewish immigration from Eastern Europe

1882   The "Treif Banquet"

1885   Pittsburgh Platform of Reform Judaism

1886   Founding of the Conservative movement's Jewish Theological Seminary

1889   Henrietta Szold's Russian Night School established

1903   Kishinev Massacre

1909   Founding of the New York Kehillah

1911   The Triangle Shirtwaist Company Fire

1912   *The Promised Land* by Mary Antin published

1913   Founding of the Anti-Defamation League by B'nai B'rith to combat anti-Semitism

1915   Lynching of Leo Frank in Georgia

1916   Confirmation of Louis Brandeis as associate justice of the United States Supreme Court

1922   First Bat Mitzvah, of Judith Kaplan

1927   Release of the film *The Jazz Singer*

1933   Hitler comes to power in Germany

1942   The Riegner telegram

1948   Proclamation of the State of Israel

1967   Six-Day War

1972   Ordination of Sally Priesand as first woman rabbi

1979   Peace Treaty signed between Israel and Egypt

1985   The Jonathan Pollard affair

1993   Opening of the United States Holocaust Museum in Washington, D.C.

2000   Nomination of Senator Joseph Lieberman as the Democratic Party candidate for vice president of the United States

Selected Bibliography

Bernstein, Philip. *To Dwell in Unity. The Jewish Federation Movement in America Since 1960.* Philadelphia: The Jewish Publication Society, 1983.

Dash, Joan. *Summoned to Jerusalem.* New York: Harper, 1979.

Dinnerstein, Leonard. *The Leo Frank Case.* New York: Columbia University Press, 1968.

Finkelstein, Norman H. *Friends Indeed: The Special Relationship of Israel and the United States.* Brookfield, Conn.: The Millbrook Press, 1998.

Finkelstein, Norman H. *Heeding the Call: Jewish Voices in America's Civil Rights Struggle.* Philadelphia: The Jewish Publication Society, 1997.

Fishman, Sylvia Burack. *Jewish Life and American Culture.* Albany, N. Y.: State University of New York Press, 2000.

Freedman, Samuel. *Jew vs. Jew.* New York: Simon and Schuster, 2000.

Gilman, Neil. *Conservative Judaism.* New York: Behrman House, 1993.

Goldberg, J. J. *Jewish Power.* Reading, Mass.: Addison-Wesley, 1996.

Golden, Harry. *The Lynching of Leo Frank.* New York: Cassell, 1966.

Goren, Arthur A. *New York Jews and the Quest for Community*. New York: Columbia University Press, 1970.

Goren, Arthur A., ed. *Dissenter in Zion*. Cambridge: Harvard University Press, 1962.

Howe, Irving. *World of Our Fathers*. New York: Schocken Books, 1989.

Lurie, Harry. L. *A Heritage Affirmed*. Philadelphia: The Jewish Publication Society, 1961.

Meltzer, Milton. *Starting From Home*. New York: Viking, 1979.

Moore, Deborah Dash. *At Home in America*. New York: Columbia University Press, 1981.

Rischin, Moses. *The Promised City*. Cambridge: Harvard University Press, 1977.

Stein, Leon. *The Triangle Fire*. New York: Lippincott, 1962.

Whitfield, Stephen S. *In Search of American Jewish Culture*. Hanover, N. H.: Brandeis University Press, 1999.

Wood, E. Thomas and Stanislaw M. Jankowski. *How One Man Tried to Stop the Holocaust*. New York: Wiley, 1994.

Index

A

Abzug, Bella, 156–157
adult education, 114–115
Anti-Defamation League
   continuing monitoring efforts of
      bigotry, 136
   founding, 70
   opposing bigotry, 78
anti-Semitism. *see* bigotry
Antin, Mary, 91–92, 106
Ashkenazic Judaism, 3
assimilation
   declining Jewish population, 186
   life in suburbs, 13–14
authors, 91–96
   Antin, Mary, 91–92
   Cahan, Abraham, 93
   Miller, Arthur, 92
   Roth, Philip, 93
   Simon, Neil, 96

B

baseball players, 99–101
Beilis, Mendel, 58
Benjamin, Judah, 59
Berkman, Alexander, 30
Berle, Milton, 84
Bernstein, Leonard, 182

bigotry
   Bingham, Theodore, 47
   continued monitoring of, 135–136
   Coughlin, Father Charles, 75
   current status of, 184–186
   decline of after WWII, 131
   Duke, David, 77
   Ford, Henry, 70–74
   Frank, Leo, lynching of, 60–69
   in early America, 57
   Ku Klux Klan, 77
   Lindbergh, Charles A., 74
   reasons for, 58
   Watson, Thomas E., 62
Brandeis, Louis D., 25, 168–171

C

Cahan, David, 93
Cantor, Eddie, 39–43
Cardozo, Benjamin, 170
cloakmakers' strike, 25–26
comedians, 97–98
comic books, 97
Conservative Judaism
   founding, 7
   Jewish Theological Seminary, 7
   ordination of women rabbis,
      157–159

D

Conservative Judaism, *continued*
  Treif Banquet, 7
  Women's league for, 155
Coolidge, Calvin, 15
Coughlin, Father Charles, 75

day schools, 111–113
Democratic Party, Jewish support for, 33, 177
Dreyfus affair, 58
Dubinsky, David, 58
Duke, David, 31

E

Eastern Europe, attitude toward Jews, 1
education
  alternatives, 113–114
  conflicts with modern life, 110
  day schools, 111–113
  for adults, 114–115
  future needs, 188–189
  heder, 107–108
  improving level of, 109
  Jewish studies in universities, 112, 115

F

federations, 53–55
feminism
  Abzug, Bella, 156–157
  Ginsburg, Ruth, 156, 165–168
  ordination of women rabbis, 157–160
  women in traditional roles, 154
Ford, Henry, 70–74
Frank, John, 101
Frank, Leo, 60–69

G

gays, role in Judaism, 160–162
German-Jewish immigration, 3
Ginsburg, Ruth, 156, 165–168
Goldberg, Bill, 100

Goldman, Emma, 30, 32–33
Gompers, Samuel, 22
Gore, Al, 145
Great Revolt, The, 25
Greenberg, Hank, 99

H

havurot, 13
Hebrew
  teaching of, 110
  use of in prayers, 4
Hebrew Union College, 5
heder, 107–108
Heschel, Rabbi Abraham Joshua, 34
Hollywood studios, 85–86, 91
Holocaust
  as substitute for religion, 145
  description of concentration camp, 120
  Israel as response to, 130
  Kristallnacht, 123
  museums commemorating, 134
  Quanza, 124–126
  Reigner telegram, 118–119
  rise of Nazis, 122–123
  St. Louis, 122–124
  US immigration policy after, 133
  US immigration policy during, 126
  US Jews' attitudes during WWII, 128–129
  War Refugee Board, 130–131
  Wise, Rabbi Stephen S. warns of, 118–121

I

ILGWU (International Ladies Garment Workers Union), 19
immigrants
  attending night school, 104–105
  harsh life, 43–47
  Hollywood studios, 85
  Kehilla experiment, 48–52
  Lower East Side, 37–39
  working in sweatshops, 17–18

describing life of workers, 26
Levine, Charles A., 81, 82
Lieberman, Joseph, 163–164, 165, 176, xi–xii
Lindbergh, Charles A., 74
Lower East Side, 37–39

M

Magnes, Rabbi Judah, 48–50
Marshall, Louis
 attacks on by Henry Ford, 72
 founding of Kehillah, 48
Mendelssohn, Moses, 3
Miller, Arthur, 92
Moskowitz, Belle, 31

N

National Book Award, 86
National Council of Young Israel, 9
National Pencil Company, 60
National Yiddish Book Center, 90
Nazis. see Holocaust
night school, 104–105

O

Orthodox Judaism, 1
 attitude toward Israel, 141
 day schools, 111
 differences within Orthodoxy, 12
 isolationism, 12
 monopoly over religious life in Israel, 151–152
National Council of Young Israel, 9
Soloveitchik, Rabbi Joseph, 10
 tensions with Reform Jews, 5–6

P

Perkins, Frances, 28
Phagan, Mary, 60–61
politics, Jewish involvement in, 171–179
Pollard, Jonathan Jay, 150
population centers, Jewish, 186
prejudice against Jews. see bigotry
Pulitzer Prize, 86

immigration. see also bigotry; immigrants
 assistance to Eastern European Jews, 5
 from Germany, 3
 need to adapt American ways, 7
 US policy after Holocaust, 133
 US policy during Holocaust, 126
Israel
 American Jewish support for, 142–149
 as solution to Holocaust, 132
 as source of Jewish connection, 152
 as substitute for religion, 145
 declining emphasis on, 187–188
 reduced emphasis on fundraising, 148–149
 Six-Day War, 137–140
 Yom Kippur War, 146 147

J

Jewish causes, trend toward, 15–16
Jewish education. see education
Jewish Labor Committee, 31
Jewish Theological Seminary, 7
 admission of Henrietta Szold, 154
Jewish Welfare Board, 54
Jolson, Al, 80–85

K

Karski, Jan, 121
Kehilla, 48–52
 attacks on by Henry Ford, 72
Jewish education, 109
King, Rev. Martin Luther, Jr., 34, 35
Kishinev, pogrom in, 58
Kissinger, Henry, 146
Koufax, Sandy, 99
Kristallnacht, 123
Ku Klux Klan, 77

L

Landsmanshaften (self-help organizations), 46–47
Lansky, Meyer, 51
Lemlich, Clara, 20, 25

Q

Quanza, 124–126

R

radio programs, 88–91
Reform Judaism
  attitude toward Israel, 141
  Declaration of Principles, 4
  Mendelssohn, Moses, 3–4
  ordination of women rabbis, 159
  tensions with Orthodox Jews, 5–6
Riegner Telegram, 118–119
Roosevelt, Eleanor, and *Quanza* affair,
  125
Roosevelt, Franklin D., 33
Rosenthal, Herman "Beansey," 49
Roth, Philip, 93

S

Schneiderman, Rose, 31
Seinfeld, Jerry, 184
Shabbat Across America program, 10,
  14–15
shirtwaist workers' strike, 20–25
Simon, Neil, 96
Six-Day War, 137–140
Slaton, John, 66–67
Soloveitchik, Rabbi Joseph, 10
Specter, Arlen, 174, 175
sports, 99–101
St. Louis, 123–124
Streisand, Barbara, 98
sweatshops
  hours and wages, 23
  life of workers, 17–19, 26
  Triangle Shirtwaist Company fire,
    27–29
Szold, Henrietta
  admission to Jewish Theological
    Seminary, 154
  educating immigrants, 105

T

Tenement Museum, 45
The Jazz Singer, 82–85
Treif Banquet, 7
Triangle Shirtwaist Company fire, 25–29
  resulting safety legislation, 30
Truman, Harry, 142, 143, 151

U

Union of American Hebrew
  Congregations, 4
unions, 30–31
Uprising of the Twenty Thousand, 25, 28

V

vaudeville, 87–88

W

War Refugee Board, 130–131
Watson, Thomas, 62, 67, 68
Wise, Rabbi Stephen S.
  attitude toward Zionism, 142
  discovery of Holocaust, 118
  efforts against Holocaust, 122, 129
  Quanza affair, 124–125
women. *see* feminism
workers' rights, 19–31
Workmen's Circle, 31

Y

Yeshiva University, 10
Yiddish, 2–3
  rediscovery of, 90
Yom Kippur War, 146–147

Z

Zionism. *see* Israel